# CRITICAL ACCLAIM FOR THE WORKS OF JAMES RADA, JR.

*Saving Shallmar*

"But Saving Shallmar's Christmas story is a tale of compassion and charity, and the will to help fellow human beings not only survive, but also be ready to spring into action when a new opportunity presents itself. Bittersweet yet heartwarming, Saving Shallmar is a wonderful Christmas season story for readers of all ages and backgrounds, highly recommended."

*Small Press Bookwatch*

*Battlefield Angels*

"Rada describes women religious who selflessly performed life-saving work in often miserable conditions and thereby gained the admiration and respect of countless contemporaries. In so doing, Rada offers an appealing narrative and an entry point into the wealth of sources kept by the sisters."

*Catholic News Service*

*Between Rail and River*

"The book is an enjoyable, clean family read, with characters young and old for a broad-based appeal to both teens and adults. Between Rail and River also provides a unique, regional appeal, as it teaches about a particular group of people, ordinary working 'canawlers' in a story that goes beyond the usual coverage of life during the Civil War."

*Historical Fiction Review*

*Canawlers*

"A powerful, thoughtful and fascinating historical novel, Canawlers documents author James Rada, Jr. as a writer of considerable and deftly expressed storytelling talent."

*Midwest Book Review*

"James Rada, of Cumberland, has written a historical novel for high-schoolers and adults, which relates the adventures, hardships and ultimate tragedy of a family of boaters on the C&O Canal. ... The tale moves quickly and should hold the attention of readers looking for an imaginative adventure set on the canal at a critical time in history."

*Along the Towpath*

**OTHER BOOKS BY JAMES RADA, JR.**

*Fiction*

    Beast

    Between Rail and River

    Canawlers

    Kachina

    Kuskurza

    Logan's Fire

    My Little Angel

    The Race

    The Rain Man

    October Mourning

*Non-Fiction*

    Battlefield Angels: The Daughters of Charity Work as Civil War Nurses

    Kidnapping the General: The South's Most-Daring Raid Against the Union Army

    Looking Back: True Stories of Mountain Maryland

    Looking Back II: More True Stories of Mountain Maryland

    Saving Shallmar: Christmas Spirit in a Coal Town

    When the Babe Came to Town: Stories of George Herman Ruth's Small-Town Baseball Games

# NO NORTH, NO SOUTH...

The Grand Reunion at the 50th Anniversary of the Battle of Gettysburg

by

James Rada, Jr.

PUBLISHING

NO NORTH, NO SOUTH...:
THE GRAND REUNION AT THE 50TH ANNIVERSARY OF THE BATTLE OF GETTYSBURG

Published by Legacy Publishing, a division of AIM Publishing Group.
Gettysburg, Pennsylvania.
Copyright © 2013 by James Rada, Jr.
All rights reserved.
Printed in the United States of America.
Second printing: June 2013.

ISBN 0-9714599-8-3

315 Oak Lane • Gettysburg, Pennsylvania 17325

# CONTENTS

Henry S. Huidekoper
7

The Pennsylvania Battle of Gettysburg Commission
12

Arriving
29

Veterans' Day - July 1, 1913
56

Military Day - July 2, 1913
68

Civic Day - July 3, 1913
77

National Day - July 4, 1913
92

Goodbyes
96

Epilogue
101

Endnotes
104

*"This occasion declares, when we come to consider our nation and future, that there is no North, no South, no East, no West, but simply a great Republic which finds in the spirit of its people patriotic pride, unchanging loyalty, and unfailing devotion to the highest principles of human liberty."*

*- Bennett Young, United Confederate Veterans*
*Speaking at the 50th anniversary of the Battle of Gettysburg*

GAR veterans at the Grand Reunion at Gettysburg, 1913. *(Courtesy of the Library of Congress)*

# 1

# HENRY S. HUIDEKOPER

People sometimes say that they lose themselves in their dreams. For them, it is a metaphor to explain a particularly vivid dream. When Henry Shippen Huidekoper said it; however, he meant it literally. On those evenings, his dreams turned to nightmares where he lost himself, at least part of himself.

The dream would begin happily enough. He was a young man, 23 years old and fresh out of Harvard College and serving his country as a lieutenant colonel with the 150th Pennsylvania Volunteer Infantry, "The Pennsylvania Bucktails." He took pride in his service and his accomplishment in becoming a lieutenant colonel at such a young age. In those days, it was his real life that had been the dream. He was young and patriotic and had no clue about the horrors of war.

During the morning of July 1, 1863, the worst thing Henry had to worry about was what his men would eat for breakfast. They hadn't seen their commissary wagon in a couple days. It hadn't caught up with them yet, and the men's stomachs were missing it loudly. The officers had no way to feed nearly 400 hungry men at their camp near Emmitsburg, Md., just below the Mason-Dixon Line on the road to Gettysburg, Pa. Some of the officers wanted to buy a sheep from a nearby farmer, slaughter it and roast it for a meal. While roast mutton sounded like a delicious breakfast, the talk in camp was that the regiment would move out early that morning. With little time to eat, the soldiers' complaining stomachs would once again have to be satisfied with coffee and the appropriately named hardtack that would sit heavily and slowly digest in their stomachs.[1] For some, these meager rations would be their last meal.

Soldiers from various regiments, including the 150th Pennsylvania, started marching toward Gettysburg, Pa., at 8 a.m. Lieutenant Colonel Thomas Chamberlin wrote in his history of the Pennsylvania Bucktails:

> "On either hand long stretches of golden grain and luxuriant growths of corn looked beautiful in the sunlight,

# "Lumbermen With A Wildcat Yell"

Major Roy Stone

The 13th Pennsylvania Reserves came from Pennsylvania's "Wildcat District" by raft, rowboat, horse and cattle cars to join the Union Army in the spring of 1861. They were known as excellent sharpshooters and skirmishers.

The regiment was called the Bucktailed Wildcats. The term "bucktail" came from the soldiers' custom of wearing the tail of a deer he had shot. "Wildcats" came from the young lumbermen being a wild and boisterous group.

While Confederate soldiers were known for their wild and loud Rebel Yell, the Pennsylvania Bucktails were largely made up of young lumbermen who had their own Wildcat Yell.

So quickly did their reputation grow that Secretary of War Edwin Stanton asked that additional Bucktails be raised in July 1862. Maj. Roy Stone raised 20 additional companies. The companies were organized into the 149th and 150th Pennsylvania Regiments in August 1862. These new regiments called themselves the "Bucktails."

and it was hard to believe that this armed host was approaching the scene of a battle. Soon, however, citizens were met driving cattle and horses before them in search of a safe retreat, and when, a little later, two children - a boy and a girl - rode past on one horse, crying as if their little hearts would break, it was painfully apparent that the miseries of war had penetrated to this hitherto quiet pastoral region."[2]

That didn't bode well for the soldiers. They were marching toward something from which other people were running.

Before the soldiers could reach Gettysburg, a staff officer with new orders galloped up to them on his horse. Part of the army on the Emmitsburg Road veered off to march double time to a location southwest of the Lutheran Theological Seminary.

"The exertion proved too great for many of the men, and quite a number of the 150th were compelled to fall out of the ranks. Captain Dougal, of Company D, the largest and most corpulent officer in the regiment, found himself unequal to the telling pace, and, having asked permission to drop behind, was instructed to gather up the stragglers and bring them to the front,-an order which he executed most satisfactorily."³

Colonel Langhorne Wister, commander of the 150th Pennsylvania, received instructions on where to position the regiment and ordered the soldiers to pile their knapsacks on the ground so as not to weigh them down unnecessarily on their charge.

"Forward!" he commanded the regiment, forgetting that he hadn't had them load their muskets.

The men quickly yelled to Col. Wister that their weapons weren't loaded. So the men stopped and readied their muskets. Then their regimental colors were unfurled and 150th headed westward to a hill that overlooked Willoughby Run.⁴

The 149th and 143rd Pennsylvania took up positions to the right that extended the line to Chambersburg Road. They could see dead and wounded soldiers scattered across the field to the rear of their line.

The men of the 150th remained hunkered down for an hour as the Confederate Army shelled their position. Colonel Roy Stone, commander of the 149th Pennsylvania, was severely wounded. Wister left to command the 149th, but not before giving Lt. Col. Huidekoper command of the 150th.

Col. Wister returned for a short time to make some adjustments to the lines and the 150th waited for an expected rebel attack. A Confederate regiment was trying to flank the 143rd and 149th Regiments, which had already repulsed a frontal assault.

Col. Wister then led a charge that routed the Rebels and allowed the regiment to recapture the colors of the 149th Pennsylvania. However, the Rebel attack gained even greater ferocity and they forced the 150th to fall back. The Union soldiers fought valiantly, but wavered as they struggled to hold their position.

Amid the fighting, Lt. Col. Huidekoper was wounded in his leg with a minie ball that cut to the bone. The wound was treated and Huidekoper fought on only to have his right arm shattered by another ball.⁵

"Lieutenant-Colonel Huidekoper, as soon as his broken arm could be hurriedly cared for, returned to the line, which continued to be maintained in the face of discouraging odds; but pain and faintness from shock and loss of blood presently compelled him to retire."⁶

Henry Shippen Huidekoper during the Civil War. *(Courtesy of Homeoftheheroes.com)*

His arm wound was so serious that when he was taken into Gettysburg that evening, the doctors quickly decided as they often did, that amputation was necessary. It was a treatment that many soldiers feared as much as enemy fire since it was deadlier. The primary mortality rate from amputation was 28 percent and the secondary amputation mortality rate was 52 percent.⁷

Lt. Col. Huidekoper lost his arm to the

Langhorne Wister as a general in the army. *(Courtesy of LaSalle University)*

surgeon's bonesaw. Where the limb wound up is unknown unlike General Dan Sickles' leg, which would still be on display 150 years later. Most likely Huidekoper's limb was buried in a pit along with hundreds of other amputated limbs.

The loss of his arm changed Henry Huidekoper's life. He survived the surgery after a long recovery, but he was forced to turn down command of the 150th Pennsylvania in 1864 because the wound never fully healed. Huidekoper lived, though, which was important when so many other soldiers weren't so lucky.

He had left a part of himself at Gettysburg. It gave him a strong connection to the battlefield almost as if it was a part of himself. He visited there frequently after the war and walked the ground he had marched years earlier. He probably even wondered where his arm had come to rest and if he was walking on his own grave or rather the grave for his arm. So much blood had been spilled at Gettysburg. So many lives had been lost. Here the course of the war, and indeed, the nation had changed. It was truly hallowed ground.

As Huidekoper grew older, he attended some of the reunions and gatherings of Civil War veterans. Each year seemed to bring a softening of the animosity between the Confederate and Union veterans. Though the Union and Confederate states had proclaimed peace in 1865, true peace would not be won until it was felt in the hearts of each veteran. Huidekoper could feel that time was approaching.

"Surprisingly, reconciliation after this great cataclysm probably began first among the veterans themselves," author James W. Wensyel once wrote.[8]

Huidekoper wanted it to be sooner rather than later because by the 20th Century, it was hard not to notice was that the number of Civil War veterans were decreasing as they passed away. The remaining veterans were aging into their sixties at a time when the average lifespan of American was around 47 years.[9]

In April 1908, he was speaking with Pennsylvania Governor Edwin Stuart and mentioned that with the upcoming 50th anniversary of the Civil War, the State of Pennsylvania should undertake to remember its role in the war. A reunion of former enemies should be planned at Gettysburg to put aside any previous animosity and simply honor the veterans who were no longer alive. Huidekoper recommended both sides be invited to once and for all lay aside enmity.

He had planted a seed and it began to grow.

# The Battle of Gettysburg

|  | *Union Army* | *Confederate Army* |
|---|---|---|
| **Commander** | General George Meade | General Robert E. Lee |
| **Strength** | 93,921 | 71,699 |
| **Killed** | 3,155 | 4,078 |
| **Wounded** | 14,531 | 12,693 |
| **Captured/Missing** | 5,369 | 5,830 |

Pennsylvania Governor Edwin Stuart who first introduced the idea of a 50th battle reunion at Gettysburg to the Pennsylvania legislature in his 1909 biennial address. *(Courtesy of Wikimedia Commons)*

Henry S. Huidekoper at the time of the 50th Gettysburg Reunion. *(Scanned from the Pennsylvania Reunion Commission Report)*

# 2

# THE PENNSYLVANIA BATTLE OF GETTYSBURG COMMISSION

As Gov. Stuart pondered Henry Huidekoper's comments and idea, he began thinking that a grand reunion was something that Pennsylvania could organize to honor the aging veterans of the Civil War.

He wasn't the only one recognizing that time was growing short to honor veterans from the War Between the States. Lieutenant Colonel John P. Nicholson, who served as chairman of the Gettysburg National Park Commission called a meeting with the citizens of Gettysburg on Sept. 8, 1908, to talk about the town's ability to support a grand reunion of Civil War veterans on the 50th anniversary of the battle. Following his remarks, he took residents' questions, concerns and support to the governor on Oct. 15.[1]

Gettysburg had hosted battlefield reunions before, but they were relatively small events. In 1878, the Grand Army of the Republic had an encampment on East Cemetery Hill during which the first monuments outside of the Soldiers' National Cemetery were laid.[2] Just a few years previous, veterans of the Philadelphia Brigade and Pickett's Division had met on the battlefield in 1906 and Confederate Brigadier General Lewis Armistead's captured sword had been returned to his men.

> "It has been having reunions, celebrations, controversies, processions, dedications, speeches, big and little and without number, for forty years. Privates, Lieutenants, Captains, Majors, Colonels, Generals, Governors, all look alike to Gettysburg. It has been surfeited. Nothing less than a President of the United States or a fire can cause it to become agitated—with the odds in favor of the fire."[3]

For this milestone reunion, people envisioned an immense event with so many people in town and the surrounding countryside as hadn't been seen since the battle itself. For such a reunion, preparations would have to begin early since any infrastructure improvements could take some time to complete.

Gov. Stuart gave his bi-ennial message to the Pennsylvania state legislature on January 5, 1909. He explained that the 50th anniversary of the Civil War was approaching and that the commonwealth had sent 69 infantry regiments, 10 cavalry regiments and seven artillery batteries to fight and die in the war. Stuart said:

> "Many of the men of these commands are still living, and many will be living on the fiftieth anniversary of the battle, and it would be entirely in keeping with the patriotic spirit of the people of the Commonwealth to properly recognize and fittingly observe this anniversary. Other States, both north and south, whose sons fought at Gettysburg, will surely co-operate in making the occasion one that will stand foremost in the martial history of the world."[4]

## THE PENNSYLVANIA REUNION COMMISSION

The state senators and representatives agreed with Gov. Stuart and unanimously passed a law on May 13 that created a state commission with the sole goal of planning the 50th anniversary of the Battle of Gettysburg.

The legislature also approved an $5,000 to cover the commission's initial expenses.

The governor appointed the members of the commission in August 1909. They were all Civil War veterans and members of the Grand Army of the Republic. The members were:
- Louis Wagner of Philadelphia, Colonel in the 88th Regular Pennsylvania Volunteer Infantry and brevet brigadier general in the U.S. Volunteers.
- John R. Brooke of Philadelphia, Major general with the U.S. Army Retired.
- R. Dale Benson of Philadelphia, 1st lieutenant with the 114th Pennsylvania Volunteer Infantry and brevet major with the U.S. Volunteers.
- R. Bruce Ricketts of Wilkes-Barre, Major and brevet colonel with the 1st Pennsylvania Artillery.
- J. Richard Boyle of Reading, Adjutant with the 111th Pennsylvania Volunteer Infantry and captain A.Q. M. with the U.S. Army Volunteers.
- William Penn Lloyd of Mechanicsburg, Adjutant with the 1st Pennsylvania Calvary.
- Alexander McDowell of Sharon, Sergeant with the 121st Pennsylvania Volunteer Infantry and brevet major.
- Irvin. K Campbell of Pittsburgh, Corporal with the 9th Pennsylvania Reserves.
- Lewis T. Brown of Pittsburgh, Private with the 102nd Pennsylvania Volunteer Infantry.

The commission met for the first time in Philadelphia at the end of November. Wagner was elected chairman and the headquarters

The Great Camp at Gettysburg. *(Courtesy of the Library of Congress)*

# The First Southern State Monument at Gettysburg

Frederick W. Sievers

In 1911, the Commonwealth of Virginia appropriated $50,000 for a monument on the Gettysburg battlefield. It would be the first monument erected by a southern state at Gettysburg.

Frederick W. Sievers won the contract to build the monument with a design that won out over 40 other competitors. The monument design featured seven figures that represented three branches of the army during the Battle of Gettysburg – artillery, cavalry and infantry. They were on a pedestal on which was surmounted a statue of Confederate General Robert E. Lee astride his horse, Traveler.

"I have selected the characters from men of different degrees of social standing because I wanted to recall the fact that patriotism places rich and poor, the aristocrat and the son of the soil, on equal footing," Sievers said. "The most interesting feature, from my point of view, is the departure from the stereotyped manner in representing the arms of service with the usual figures in meaningless poses on different sides of the pedestal, and I believe that my treatment of the subject is original."[5]

Sievers had studied at the Royal Academy of Fine Arts in Rome, Italy, and the Académie Julian in Paris, France.

He created the figure of Lee from photographs and life masks of the general. He even travelled to Lexington, Va., to study Traveler's skeleton, which was preserved at Washington and Lee University.[6]

The Virginia Memorial is the largest Confederate monument at Gettysburg. It stands 41 feet tall. The Gen. Lee and Traveler sculpture is 14 feet tall.

When it became apparent that the monument wouldn't be ready in time for the Grand Reunion, the granite pedestal without the sculptures was dedicated on June 30, 1913. The completed monument was dedicated on June 8, 1917, and unveiled by Virginia Carter, a niece of Robert E Lee. Virginia Governor Henry C. Stuart presented the completed memorial to the Assistant Secretary of War.

(*Photos courtesy of Wikimedia Commons*)

was established in the Third National Bank in the city. The following month the commission sent out its first notice to all of the states, commonwealths and territories announcing its plan to put together a grand reunion at Gettysburg and asking for their participation and input in planning the event.[7]

The commission also urged the states to follow Pennsylvania's lead in helping its veterans attend the reunion. Besides paying to the cost of the reunion, the Pennsylvania legislature had agreed to pay for rail transportation to get any of the state's veterans to the reunion once they were inside Pennsylvania's borders.

As letters returned from the states, the response to the idea was positive and representatives were appointed from every state. They would serve as liaisons between their respective states and the Pennsylvania Battle of Gettysburg Commission.

## THE FEDERAL GOVERNMENT GETS INVOLVED

With national support, the Pennsylvania Commission hoped that the U.S. government would participate in the anniversary and offset some of the increasing costs.

Seeing the national interest in the event, the U.S. Congress passed an act in June 1910 to appoint a committee of three U.S. senators and three congressmen to confer with the Pennsylvania Commission. The federal commission would then report back "as to the proper action to be taken by Congress to enable the United States fittingly to joining in the celebration of the Fiftieth Anniversary of the Battle of Gettysburg..."[8] Congress also agreed to contribute to the commission's expenses out of the House and Senate contingency funds up to $1,000.

The men appointed to the federal commission were:

- Senator Geo. T. Olliver, chairman (Pennsylvania)
- Senator Weldon B. Heyburn (Idaho)
- Senator Isidor Rayner (Maryland)
- Representative James A. Tawney, vice chairman (Minnesota)
- Representative Daniel F. Lafean (Pennsylvania)
- Representative John Lamb (Virginia).
- Senator Claude A. Swanson (Virginia) replaced Heyburn when he resigned soon after his appointment to the commission.

On Oct.13 and 14, all of the various representatives involved with planning for the 50th anniversary were invited to a general conference in Gettysburg to "consider and agree upon the general scope and plans of the celebration."[9] Most of the state representatives were able to attend and the commission got started with planning the details of the reunion.

Obviously, the reunion would be held on the anniversary days of the battle, but the conference attendees also added July 4 as part of the event. This allowed for a general reunion called a "Peace Jubilee" and a cornerstone for a "Peace Memorial" would be laid on the nation's Independence Day. A list of speakers, including whoever was the President of the United States at the time of the reunion was drawn up. The commission also began examining issues with transportation into Gettysburg.

As for accommodations for the tens of thousands of veterans expected to attend, a tent camp was planned that would allow the veterans to be grouped by state. The commission wanted to get federal help with the equipment including getting the army to help with discipline and policing. Plans were also made for states to try and help with transportation to the event.

## THE PLANNING BEGINS

Though the 50th anniversary was still more than three years away, it was not too early to begin planning. Gettysburg had grown from about 2,400 residents in 1863 to 4,500 in 1913, but it was still too small of a town to house all of the veterans and visitors who were expected for the anniversary event.

During his bi-ennial message to the Pennsylvania Legislature on January 3, 1911, Gov. Stuart pointed out that one of the goals of the event was to "intensify the feeling of brotherhood that insures to us a united country."[10]

Water towers were constructed specially for supplying water to the residents of Great Camp during the reunion. (*Courtesy of the Library of Congress*)

The Pennsylvania Legislature also showed its commitment to making the event special by allocating another $50,000 for the expenses. Following this action, other states began debating what they could contribute to either the event itself or ensuring that its Civil War veterans could attend.

> "Though his request did not fall on deaf ears, the expense of sending hundreds of old soldiers to the reunion from as far away as California was overwhelming and many states could not provide cash donations either to the reunion or to their veterans. A handful of northern states were suc-

cessful in passing special legislation to assist their veterans while others depended on personal contributions to help get the old men to Pennsylvania. The Virginia chapter of *The United Daughters of the Confederacy* took an active role and supplied United Confederate Veterans' uniforms to those in the state who needed them. Other chapters of the UDC held socials and fund raisers to gather money for transportation as well as food, clothing, and medical assistance."[11]

At the end of January, the Pennsylvania legislature voted to provide transportation to and from Gettysburg to Civil War veterans in the state who were attending the reunion.

One of the issues that the reunion would have to deal with was that the veterans who would be attending would generally be in their 70's. For many of them, their health would be

## Camp by the Numbers

| | |
|---|---|
| 47.5 | The miles of avenues and company streets built in the reunion area. |
| 500 | Arc lights needed to light the camp. |
| 32 | Bubbling water fountains provided water throughout the camp. |
| 6,592 | Lanterns were used in the tents to provided light. |
| 13,200 | Wash basins used by residents of the camp during their stay. |
| almost 54,000 | Souvenir mess kits (each contained a knife, fork, large spoon, small spoon, tin cup and two plates) provided to each veteran. |
| 6,592 | Tents housed camp residents. |
| 44,850 | Cots were used in the tents. |
| 6,486 | Mattresses distributed to residents of the camp. |
| 6,600 | Mattress covers distributed to residents of the camp. |
| 2,070 | Bed sacks used by residents of the camp. |
| 105,262 | Blankets used by residents of the camp. |
| 90 | Miles of wire used by the Signal Corps for telephone communications. |
| 87 | Army telephones installed in the camp. |
| 7,000 to 8,000 | Daily number of calls handled using the camp telephones. |
| 35 | Pay phones installed by Bell and Independent phone companies. |
| 1 | Western Union Messenger Service. |
| 1 | Temporary U.S. Post Office. |

fragile and so appropriate accommodations would need to be made.

This became apparent even among members of the Pennsylvania Reunion Commission. Two of its original members died in 1911. Lewis T. Brown died on Mar. 19 and William Penn Lloydon passed away on Sept. 20. William J. Patterson of Pittsburgh who had been a captain with the 62nd Pennsylvania Volunteer Infantry and William E. Miller of Carlisle who had been a captain with the 3rd Pennsylvania Cavalry Regiment were appointed in their place.

Pennsylvania Governor
John Tener

As interest in attending the reunion increased and the projected numbers of attendees increased, Pennsylvania Governor John Tener (who was elected in 1911) and the reunion commission ran into reality. The larger reunion meant that the costs were skyrocketing. This meant that the state legislature would have to allocate a lot more money than expected. Politically, it was becoming a problem.

"Several legislators argued that hosting two large veteran organizations without compensation was fruitless and was eventually going to put a strain on the state budget. Tener finally approached the Federal government, which agreed to step in and appropriate funds to feed and provide tents for the veterans during the encampment. Additionally, US Army personnel would support the reunion with cooks and bakers, quartermaster staff and troops to aid in crowd control. Emergency Federal money would also pay the bills for the reunion until the states could appropriate some back payments. With this assurance of aid, the Pennsylvania legislature approved half a million dollars to cover the cost of the reunion."[12]

Ninety miles of wire was strung to connect the Great Camp with the outside world with telephones available every 400 feet. *(Scanned from the Pennsylvania Reunion Commission Report)*

In January and February 1912, the Reunion Commission met with the federal commission and the War Department to begin laying out the specifics for how the reunion would be executed. The commissions had a lot of details to plan out, such as

# No North, No South...

A veteran uses one of the water fountain specially built in the Great Camp to provide fresh cold water during the Grand Reunion. *(Courtesy of the Adams County Historical Society, Gettysburg, PA)*

Ambulances unloaded to be on hand at the Gettysburg reunion to quickly transport veterans to an aid station. *(Scanned from the Pennsylvania Reunion Commission Report)*

## "A Rose By Any Other Name..."

Different organizations called the 50th Anniversary of the Battle of Gettysburg Reunion different names. Here are the official names of the reunion.

- Celebration of the 50$^{th}$ Anniversary of the Battle of Gettysburg
- Celebration of the Semi-Centenary of the Civil War Gettysburg Celebration
- Reunion Celebration at Gettysburg
- Gettysburg Peace Reunion
- Great Peace Reunion
- Great Peace Jubilee
- Golden Jubilee
- Great Reunion
- Grand Reunion
- Blue and Gray Reunion
- Grand Reunion of the Blue and the Gray on the 50$^{th}$ Anniversary of the Battle of Gettysburg

# THE PENNSYLVANIA MEMORIAL

Construction of the Pennsylvania State Memorial on the Gettysburg battlefield.

The 110-foot-tall Pennsylvania State Memorial, the largest memorial on the Gettysburg Battlefield, was completed on April 23, 1913, just in time for the Grand Reunion. It commemorates the 34,530 Pennsylvania soldiers who fought at Gettysburg. The names of the soldiers are listed on bronze tablets mounted on the monument's granite pedestal.[15]

The monument had first been proposed in 1889 as a "Pennsylvania Memorial Hall", 60 feet wide, to be built on Little Round Top.[16] The idea, proposed by Civil War Governor Andrew Curtin, would have displayed artifacts of the Pennsylvania regiments that fought at Gettysburg.

Governor James Beaver vetoed the idea. Instead, the current site of the memorial at the triangle of Hancock, Humphreys and Pleasanton avenues, was selected in 1909 as the planning for the reunion began.[17]

Architect W. Liance Cottrell won a design competition and $500 award for his memorial design.

The 100-foot-square pedestal made from North Carolina granite has four corner towers connected by arches that support a dome and observation deck. The deck can be reached by a spiral staircase in the tower. Besides the panels with soldiers' names, the walls also hold bas-relief sculptures.

The memorial contains more than 1,400 tons of broken stone, more than 1,250 tons of granite, 740 tons of sand, more than 360 tons of cement, 50 tons of steel bars and 22 tons of marble.

The structure was completed in 1910. Niche statues in the memorial were contracted in 1911 and installed in April 1913. The monument cost was $240,000.

(*Photos courtesy of Wikimedia Commons*)

how many tents would be needed, how many blankets, what and how much food would be served, sanitation, emergency care, security and transportation. In essence, they were building a temporary city on the battlefield.

From this meeting, a resolution was introduced in the U.S. Congress that outlined additional steps that would need to be taken for the reunion. The War Department estimated that it would need $358,662.84 paid by Pennsylvania to establish "The Great Camp" in Gettysburg for 40,000 veterans. This number was eventually whittled down to $300,000.[13]

The Great Camp was 280 acres of open space "starting about two hundred (200) yards from the High Water Mark Monument on the battlefield, and lying to the southwest of the town and partly upon the scene of the first day's fight, consists of 5,000 tents, regularly holding twelve (12) men each, but now to hold eight (8) veterans, each veteran being supplied with a separate cot, blanket and mess kit, (the latter to become his property), each tent to contain also two (2) hand basins, one (1) water bucket and two (2) lanterns for candles, and candles for each."[14] The main tent where many of the speeches would be made was called "The Great Tent" and was large enough to hold between 10,000 and 15,000 people under it. Meals would be served at kitchen at the end of each company street. Only hand baggage would be allowed in the camp. The camp would open on Sunday, June 29 and remain open to July 6 in order to try and avoid a crush of traffic on roads or train station.

## FOR THE UNION AND CONFEDERATE SOLDIERS

Though the intention all along had been for the reunion to include both Union and Confederate veterans, such discussions had taken place primarily among politicians and not the veterans themselves. That changed on March

A collection of thousands of lanterns for use by veterans at the Gettysburg Reunion. *(Scanned from the Pennsylvania Reunion Commission*

4, 1912, when the commander-in-chief of the Grand Army of the Republic, Harvey C. Trimble, wrote to the commander-in-chief of the United Confederate Veterans, C. Irvine Walker inviting Confederate veterans to attend the Grand Reunion. Trimble wrote in part:

> "If this event might mark the final and complete reconciliation between those of the opposing armies of fifty years ago, and the permanent establishment of harmonious and fraternal relations between the North and South, it would certainly gladden the hearts of all our countrymen. ... Let us assemble there, and meet and greet each other hand to hand and heart to heart in the spirit of true friendship and brotherhood, born out of love for the Flag and devotion to our common Country. Thus will all the wounds of our former strife be healed, as they must sometime be, that this people, as a united and vital force may effectively and mightily solve the problems of our Nation's destiny in world affairs and human progress."[18]

Near the end of August 1912, the U.S. Congress passed a bill appropriating $150,000 for reunion-related expenses and directing the War Department to begin establishing the Great Camp at Gettysburg. However, one item that had to be dropped from the reunion plans at this point was the "Peace Memorial." Congress did not authorize its funding and so plans for the "Peace Jubilee" on July 4, 1913, were dropped from the schedule of events. (It would eventually become one the events marking the 75th anniversary of the Battle of Gettysburg in 1938.)

A collection of blankets to be used by veterans at the reunion. *(Scanned from the Pennsylvania Reunion Commission Report)*

## RISING COSTS

Another expensive issue that started to become apparent was that the number of Civil War veterans expected to attend the reunion continued to rise. It passed the initial estimate of 40,000 veterans and kept increasing. The Pennsylvania Commission wrote to the U.S. Secretary of War and explained that the initial cost estimate of $300,000 would not be enough because the attendance had been underestimated.

Secretary of War Lindley M. Garrison wrote back, saying, "There are no funds available for me for this purpose, and I am positively prohibited by express Acts of Congress from incurring one dollar's worth of expenses over and above the amounts specifically appropriated for this particular purpose. Should I do so, I would not only disobey the express law, but would lay myself open both to civil and criminal liability."[19]

The Pennsylvania Legislature passed an emergency bill on June 23 allocating another $46,000 to the reunion to care for all of the veterans in excess of 40,000.[20] When all was said and done, the commonwealth contributed $450,000 to the reunion.

Other states were also stepping up to the plate to contribute money and in-kind contributions to help their Civil War veterans attend the reunion. In all, thirty-three states contributed funds or goods to the reunion for an estimated total of $1,033,000[21] (roughly $24 million in 2013).

Col. James M. Schoonmaker

## TRANSPORTATION AND SANITATION

Some work had already begun for the reunion. The Gettysburg National Park Commission had started painting avenue fencing, gun carriages, iron tablets and shells. The park also had over 700 monuments throughout it at the time. This work would actually continue right up until the Great Camp opened.

The Great Camp took two months to erect and equip in order to be prepared for the tens of thousands of veterans who would be making their way to Gettysburg.[22]

Besides finding a way to house and feed the veterans, getting them to Gettysburg in a timely matter was becoming a growing issue. The presidents of Gettysburg's railroads set themselves to dealing with the problem: Captain John P. Green, vice president of the Pennsylvania Railroad, Captain Geo. F. Baer, president of the Reading Railroad, Colonel James M. Schoonmaker, vice president of the New York Central Railroad.[23]

Gettysburg had two single-track railroads, the Reading and the Western Maryland. The Army's Quartermaster Office estimated "that the maximum capacity of these two railroads, with their present limited track facilities, and operated as separate systems, is not over 13,000 a day, and that even this rate could not be maintained for a period exceeding two or three days."[24]

This wasn't going to be enough to handle all of the veterans and visitors who would be journeying to and from Gettysburg at the end of June and beginning of July. The management of both railroad companies began working together to make improvements to the stations in town and the rail lines at their own expense so that each one was "working in perfect harmony with the other as though for one corporation instead of for rival systems."[25]

With the increasing number of visitors expected to arrive in, concerns were also arising as to whether the roads would be adequate to handle the traffic. According to the *Gettysburg Times*, more than 30,000 cars were expected to be on the roads into Gettys-

The Great Camp ready to receive guests. (*Courtesy of the Library of Congress*)

burg.[26] This represented about 10 percent of the motorized vehicles in the country at the time.[27] The trip from Washington D.C. to Gettysburg could take around four hours on a hard-packed dirt road from Gaithersburg, Md., to Urbana, Md., and a rough stone road from Emmitsburg, Md., to Gettysburg.[28]

At the camp, water was supplied by artesian wells that had been drilled in February 1913. The well water was pumped to storage containers and distributed throughout the camp via gravity. The water was cooled as it passed through coils packed in ice. Ninety latrines that could seat 3,476 people were dug as well as ninety-five kitchen cesspools.

> "The excellent sanitary arrangements that were perfected and the careful manner in which all were treated and sheltered in the Army hospitals reflect great credit on Col. Bradley and the members of the Medical Department of the Army who served under him. ... There probably has never been a camp where the different Departments of the Army worked more in harmony, or where each contributed its share to the success of the whole achievement more efficiency."[29]

## GETTING THE PRESIDENT

Almost as a preview of spirit of the reunion, Representative Thomas Heflin of Alabama became the first southerner to speak at a Gettysburg Memorial Day Service in May.[30]

At the beginning of June, President Woodrow Wilson let the Pennsylvania Reunion Commission know that he wouldn't be attending the reunion. He said that he was following a rule that he had set for himself during his first year as President that he would not accept invitations to attend public celebrations or jubilees. Instead of being in Gettysburg, the President would be spending time at his summer home in Cornish, N. H.

Former President Howard Taft was expected to attend in his place. About a week later, Taft let the commission know that he would also be unable to attend so Vice President Thomas R. Marshall was asked to be the keynote speaker.

Near the end of June, President Woodrow Wilson telegraphed Gov. John Tener that he had reconsidered his decision and would attend. The change of heart came after Rep. A. Mitchell Palmer of Pennsylvania met with the President.

Wilson's secretary Joseph Tumulty released a statement on behalf of the President:

> "The President has felt constrained to forego his chance for a few days of much-needed rest in New Hampshire next week because he feels it his duty to attend the celebration at Gettysburg on Friday, the Fourth of July."[31]

The decision was met with approval throughout the country. The *Decatur Sunday Review* noted that, "Its nation wide significance and particularly the spirit of sectional sympathy that would result from a speech by a southern born president at the reunion of the north and south."[32]

By the end of June, the preparations had been made and the camp was ready to receive its visitors and they started to arrive.

However, even as the veterans were beginning to arrive, a controversy erupted over whether Confederate flags would be allowed at the camp. Word started circulating that only the U.S. flag would be displayed at the camp and that state and battle flags and most definitely not the Confederate flag would not be allowed.

This offended many of the Confederate regiments who still had pride in their service for the Confederate States. Southern veterans started talking about boycotting a reunion that was supposed to highlight the peace between North and South.

The Pennsylvania Reunion Commission acted quickly to set the record straight that all flags would be allowed, though the U.S. flag would be the dominant one. "Topping the camp, in plain sight for miles around, is the headquarters flag. It flies from a staff eighty feet high. The flag measures thirty-six by twenty feet. It is so heavy that no breeze yet has stretched it out straight," the *New York Times* reported.[33]

This clarification satisfied most of the Confederate veterans who were upset and many of them decided to leave their Confederate States of America flags home anyway out of respect for the United States of America flag.

Confederate General E. J. Hunter said, "This is a united country, and has only one flag. The fact that the one flag is the flag carried by our war enemies 50 years ago means nothing any more. We left our sacred standards at home."[34]

With that issue put to rest, things were on track for a Grand Reunion. When the veterans arrived, they not only came with their flags, but houses in Gettysburg were draped with the American flag and some also showed the Confederate flag.

The 50th anniversary reunion of the Battle

A veterans' band ready to entertain their comrades during the Grand Reunion.
(*Courtesy of the Adams County Historical Society, Gettysburg, PA*)

of Gettysburg had captured the imagination of the nation and stirred their souls to patriotism. *The Indianapolis News* wrote:

> "There is no record of any Civil War that shows those who were at death grips meeting in common fellowship fifty years after, citizens of a country united as it never was before. The third generation after the War of the Roses in England continued to transmit to its posterity the bitterness of the strife. Long after all who had a personal part in the French Revolution were dead, its influence was felt in the politics of the country. With us after fifty years, and while there are survivors by the thousands of the greatest Civil War of history, are found brave men ready to clasp hands and fight the old battles over in comparisons of memory sweetened by honest admiration for bravery on both sides."[35]

*The Washington Post* noted:

> "It is doubtful if ever another like celebration will be possible, for, when the century mark has rolled around, practically all the men who fought in that great battle will have been laid to rest. Their children may gather at the shrine made sacred by their fathers' blood, but the coming celebration will be the only one where the real actors in that stirring drama can ever be brought on the stage for their final bow."[36]

# MEADEBORO

Even four months out from the reunion, all of the hotels in Gettysburg were booked up and many in nearby towns were quickly filling up.

The Meadeboro Company in Philadelphia leased an old orchard on the southern end of Gettysburg. The land was bounded by Taneytown Road, Baltimore Street and Steinwehr Avenue. The camp was serviced by the trolley on two sides and staffed with Red Cross personnel in case of medical emergencies.

"Everything will be done that will tend to make the patrons of Meadeboro Village comfortable. Meals of all kinds will be furnished in the Village, and quiet and rest will be assured those who need repose after the fatigues incident to witnessing the various exercises of each day," according to the brochure for the camp.[37]

Meadeboro was said to be able to house 2,000 people during the reunion. One group of tents was called "Newspaper Row." It was where the 155 journalists who were covering the reunion stayed. This area included special telegraph wires that had been run to the camp so that the journalists could submit their stories in a timely manner.[38]

The cost to stay in Meadeboro was $1.50 a night. The cost included a cot, pillow, mattress, blanket and tent.[39]

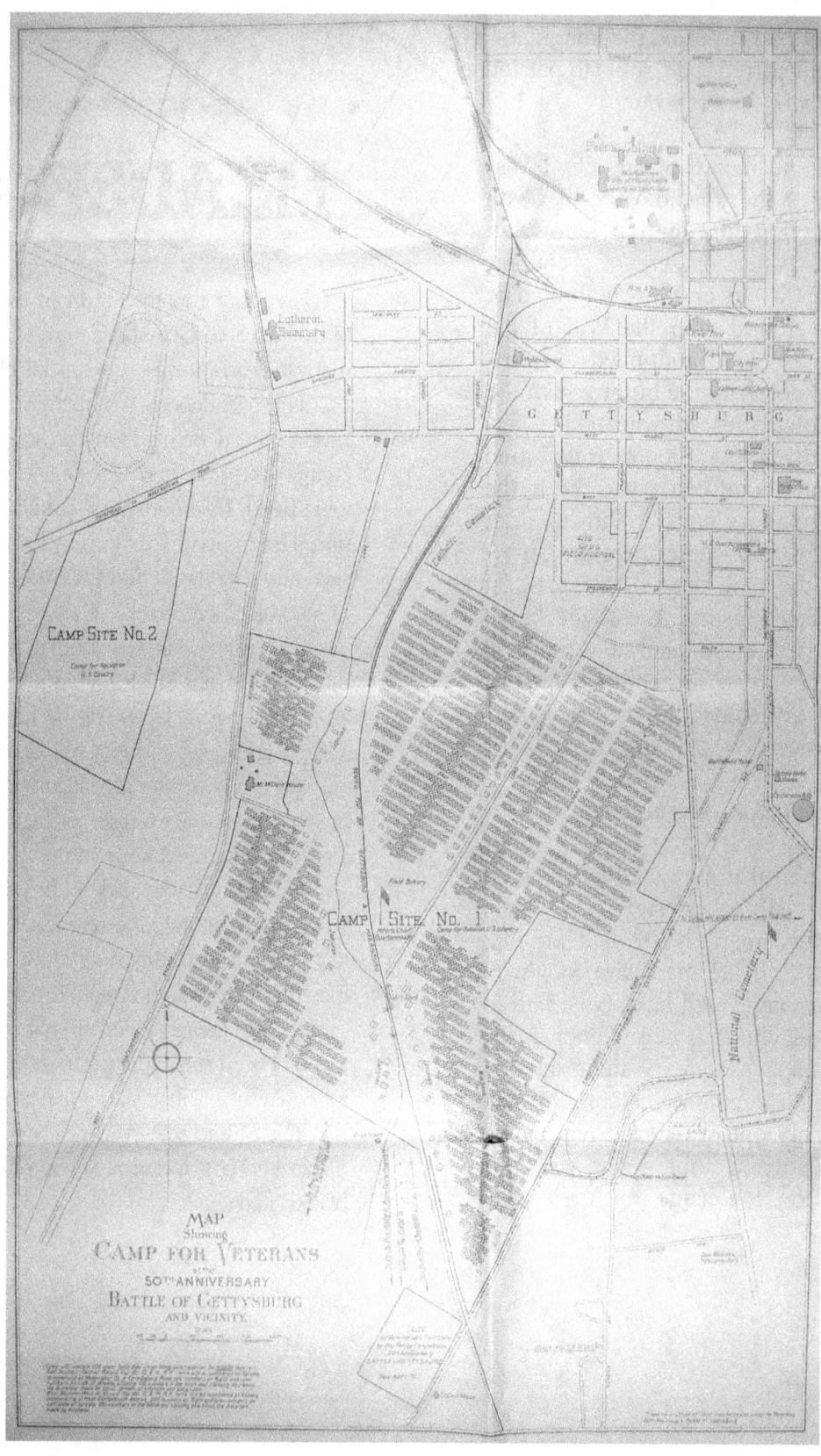

# 3

# ARRIVING

Across the country, aged Civil War veterans began preparing for the journey to Gettysburg to be part, once again, of the gathering of a great army. A newspaper reporter overheard one veteran saying, "I was talking with my wife about coming and we figured out it might be a pretty hard strain, but I said to her: 'This is most likely the last chance I'll have to do anything for the Union, and I'd like to do it fifty years from the time the Union was saved. It's going to mean something to all the younger generation to have us old fellows get together and show there isn't any hard feeling. It will take away the last excuse for the young people to cherish any sectional hatred. It's a duty we owe the country, about the last we can fill, most of us, and I figure out I ought to do it."[1]

Though the Great Camp officially opened for veterans on Sunday, June 29, early arrivals were able to find accommodations. The *New York Times* noted that on Saturday, June 28:

"Sentries, regular army privates, are patrolling the streets and avenues. The electric lights were on to-night and the band was playing. Gettysburg's 5,000 residents were in the streets. They saw men in blue and men in gray with arms over each other's shoulders or hand in hand, fighting their battles over again, but this time in a far different spirit."[2]

The first two veterans arrived for the reunion in Gettysburg for the Grand Reunion on June 26 before the camp was even open officially. William Page and William F. Brawner, two Confederate veterans of the fighting on Culp's Hill in 1863 arrived around 11 a.m. wearing their faded and worn uniforms. As they were the beginning of the South's second invasion of Gettysburg, the two men were immediately the center of attention.

"Both men were besieged immediately upon their arrival by a large party of 'boys in blue' and given the warmest sort of welcome. All during the day as they wended their way about town, the foes of fifty years ago stopped them to extend a cordial handshake and wish them the best of times during their stay here. The greeting could not have been more sincere and the men are happy as youngsters over their good time."[3]

Page and Brawner had come from the Soldiers' Home at Pikesville, Md., and had been comrades and tent mates throughout the war as members of the 2nd Maryland Regiment.

The Union soldiers who greeted them were men who were in town for a meeting of Pennsylvania veterans prior to the Grand Reunion. That reunion adjourned on June 28 and the Great Camp opened the next day.

The estimate was that 6,000 veterans would arrive on the first day that the camp was open. Instead, 21,000 veterans arrived in Gettysburg on June 29.[4] These men weren't simply veterans of the Battle of Gettysburg, but veterans from many of the great battles of the Civil War; Antietam, Manassas, Atlanta and others.

Once word had gotten out about the Grand Reunion through newspaper articles, letters from the Grand Army of the Republic and United Confederate Veterans and word of mouth, the thousands of Civil War veterans around the country took advantage of their home states' offerings to help them in various ways to get to Gettysburg.

A group of California veterans was one of the early arrivals, making use of free transportation provided by the state government.

"Sixty California Civil War veterans left for Gettysburg Thursday in a special train. While the $15,000 state appropriation to pay the transportation expenses of the veterans was declared illegal, because of a technical flaw, many of those going have had their way paid by popular subscription in their home towns."[5]

The Great Camp sits ready for the arrival of its special guests. (*Courtesy of the Library of Congress*)

Another group of veterans traveled from Genesee County, New York, and received a heroic send off.

"A group of gray-haired gentlemen marched briskly into the New York Central Station in Batavia late on Sunday afternoon, June 29, 1913, dressed in their Sunday best.

"The Batavia City Band accompanied them, playing military music. Members of various veterans groups also joined in.

"The men were local veterans of the Civil War, and Batavia was giving them a rousing sendoff. Soon the old soldiers began to board trains that transported them to a reunion honoring the 50th anniversary of the Battle of Gettysburg in Gettysburg, Pa."[6]

More than 70 Civil War veterans made the trip to Gettysburg. They were old men in their late 60's and 70's. Some of them had fought with the 8th New York Heavy Artillery Regiment. The oldest one of the group was 86-year-old William Squires of Batavia, N.Y.

Even if the veterans weren't getting any help from their states to attend the reunion, they still insisted on making the journey. John Francis Key, the grandson of Francis Scott Key, composer of *The Star-Spangled Banner,* was an 82-year-old veteran who had served in the 2nd Maryland Infantry with the Confederate State of America. He lived in Pikesville. Though not far from Gettysburg, he wasn't able to book a seat on a train to the reunion, but that didn't deter him. "Word has been brought here by two of his comrades at the home that Key had failed to get railroad transportation, but had bade them goodbye with tears streaming down his cheeks and said he would 'go to Gettysburg if he had to walk.'"[7]

The trip was 75 miles and one of Key's friends, William Page, said, "Key is a right smart man and in pretty good health, and I would not be surprised if he did walk here."[8]

Luckily, as news of his predicament leaked out, someone volunteered to drive Key to the reunion. He arrived safely and was quickly surrounded by his former comrades.

Leopold Wolf of Harrisburg wasn't as lucky. The 78-year-old Civil War veteran had few friends and no family, but he had his memories of the war and was determined to attend the reunion. He also had his pride and he was too proud to ask for a ride to the reunion and he didn't have the $1.50 fare he would have needed to pay to get to Gettysburg.

"I thought it over and decided that I would have to walk. I bought a map of the state and with the few pennies I had and started in early Saturday morning. It did not go so bad the first day, although the sun was terribly hot. The people all along the way were just as kindly as they could be to me, and that helped me a lot. I had good places to sleep, too," Wolf said.[10]

He started out on his 47-mile journey strong and energetic, but he was an old man and after sleeping in a barn the first night, he began to feel the miles in his aged body.

"I never went through worse agony in my life. About noon I could hardly hobble 20 feet without stopping for a rest, and when I finally struck the town I thought I would never get through it to the camp. When I did get in I just

### Reunion

"Mrs. Young, of North Washington Street, was surprised to receive as a caller Thursday afternoon Rev. W. F. Hubbard, of Los Angeles, California. Rev. Mr. Hubbard was wounded here and Mrs. Young was one of the young ladies of Gettysburg who helped to alleviate the sufferings of those injured in the battle. She chanced to be his nurse and he made a special call to thank her for her services."[9]

Arriving guests (clockwise from top left) Sec. of War Lindley Garrison and Gen. Hunter Liggett, Vice President Thomas Marshall and his wife, Gen. Liggett and guests, a GAR delegation from Indiana, and a pair of unidentified guests. (*Courtesy of the Library of Congress*)

# Veterans Attending by State

Forty-one of the 48 states, territories and Washington D.C. sent veterans to the Grand Reunion in 1913.[11] These numbers are taken from a *New York Times* report and while they give a good representation of the number of veterans by state who attended the 50th reunion of the Battle of Gettysburg, they do not reflect the actual number of veterans who attended the Grand Reunion during the week that the Great Camp was open.

**Confederate States**

| | |
|---|---:|
| Virginia | 1,827 |
| South Carolina | 351 |
| Georgia | 225 |
| Louisiana | 189 |
| Arkansas | 144 |
| Mississippi | 144 |
| Texas | 144 |
| North Carolina | 121 |
| Kentucky | 117 |
| Tennessee | 99 |
| *Total* | *3,361* |

**Union States**

| | |
|---|---:|
| Pennsylvania | 17,820 |
| New York | 9,692 |
| New Jersey | 1,898 |
| Massachusetts | 1,863 |
| Michigan | 900 |
| West Virginia | 810 |
| Indiana | 666 |
| Ohio | 657 |
| New Hampshire | 657 |
| Vermont | 605 |
| Maine | 603 |
| Illinois | 513 |
| Maryland* | 495 |
| Connecticut | 450 |
| Washington, DC | 405 |
| Minnesota | 396 |
| Rhode Island | 396 |
| Iowa | 378 |
| Missouri | 369 |
| Delaware | 279 |
| Wisconsin | 279 |
| South Dakota | 198 |
| California | 153 |
| Washington | 144 |
| Kansas | 117 |
| Oregon | 81 |
| Utah | 78 |
| Colorado | 72 |
| Idaho | 35 |
| North Dakota | 24 |
| Arizona | 18 |
| *Total* | *41,051* |

\* The original *New York Times* article listed Maryland as a Confederate state.

Downtown Gettysburg decked out to welcome the Civil War veterans and other visitors to the Grand Reunion. *(Courtesy of the Adams County Historical Society, Gettysburg, PA)*

sank down on the first unoccupied cot I could find and went to sleep," Wolf said.[12]

In Washington D.C., 750 veterans arrived at Union Station expecting to have tickets paid for and waiting for them. Unfortunately, when they arrived at the Hibbs Building to collect their travel expenses promised by the federal government, the $4,000 that had been promised for the veterans hadn't yet been appropriated. They had to pay for their tickets in order to get to the reunion on time and apply for reimbursement later.

The first train of Washington veterans left the station at 9 a.m. on June 29. Another left a half an hour later and the last train left the next day at 1:55 p.m.

In a show of solidarity, Union and Confederate veterans march down the street in Gettysburg. (*Courtesy of the Library of Congress*)

Colonel Thomas Hopkins who had charge of transporting the Washington veterans said that the trains into Gettysburg were booked and "have scheduled so many specials for this event that they refuse to put on one more train."[13]

As the veterans arrived in Gettysburg, they were met by Boys Scouts of America and graduates from the Tuskegee Institute in Alabama. The school, which would become famous for training African American pilots during World War II, was founded in 1881 as the Tuskegee Normal School for Colored Teachers. The Tuskegee students and scouts served as porters to carry the veterans' luggage to waiting cars that carried the luggage and some of the veterans to the camp.[14]

The town itself was decorated for the event. Businesses were draped in red, white and blue and houses proudly flew the U.S. flag. Some also flew Confederate flags.

"Large pictures of both Union and Confederate generals are much in evidence. The town is gay with martial music. Many of the veterans have brought their fifes, drums, and bugles, and the calls of wartime days are sounded through the streets, in some instances, by the very men who did the same thing during the exciting days of the

## Finding a Place to Sleep

Among the veterans who arrived in Gettysburg, was General F. M. Easton from Boston, Massachusetts. He immediately went to the Eagle Hotel to book a room. Though he was going to be in the Great Camp for most of the reunion, he wanted to spend one specific night in the Eagle Hotel.

On June 30, 1863, Easton had come to Gettysburg looking for supplies for his men. He was unable to get them that day so he stayed in the hotel that night.

Now 50 years later, he wanted to spend the night of June 30 in the same room he had stayed in on the eve of the great battle. The problem was that the room had been booked for months in advance and no amount of Easton's beseeching the hotel owner could make the room available.

One of the men who occupied the room heard Easton's pleas and volunteered to double up with another man in a different room to allow Easton's wish to become a reality.[18]

---

Two trolley cars running on the Gettysburg Railway Company's line, which ran across the battlefield, hit head-on near Devil's Den. Six passengers were injured and treated at the camp hospital.[20]

With more than 50,000 senior citizens expected to stay on the battlefield, health emergencies were expected. The men were sleeping in hot tents where the temperatures could reach over 100 degrees during the hottest part of the day and they didn't have air conditioning to stay comfortable. They would have to endure these conditions for four days or longer. Some health officials worried that there might be nearly as many casualties during the 50th reunion as there had been during the 1863 battle.

The first aid services for the veterans were set up so that "within two minutes after the discovery of illness the telephone will have carried word to the nearest regimental hospital."[21]

One of the two camp ambulances would be dispatched to pick up the ill veteran. Each ambulance could carry six passengers each.

"Less than ten minutes will elapse from the time a veteran is found to be ill until he will be in the hands of the most efficient med-

Gettysburg campaign half a century ago."[15]

Daniel Williams, who had been an 11-year-old drummer at the Battle of Fredericksburg in 1862, once again took up his drums in 1913. He was joined by George Washington Wolf, the oldest fifer of the Union Army. Together, they played a march and led the Washington D.C. veterans through town to the camp.[16]

With the Great Camp spread over 280 acres, incoming veterans were grouped by their home state. Pennsylvania and New York had the two largest state continents and they occupied the northern section of the camp along both sides of Long Lane. Veterans from other Union states had their camps between Seminary Ridge and Long Lane. Veterans from former Confederate states had their camps west of Long Lane up to the base of the monument to General Robert E. Lee.

## KEEPING VETERANS HEALTHY

The veterans arrived in Gettysburg at the peak of summer with its high temperatures

One of the North Carolina veterans' tents at the reunion. *(Scanned from the Pennsylvania Reunion Commission Report)*

A veteran points out a battle site to a pair of ladies who were helping at a aid station. *(Scanned from the Pennsylvania Reunion Commission Report)*

and high humidity. Even at daybreak, the temperatures in Gettysburg were in the eighties. Humidity remained high throughout the day during the reunion. Before the camp had even officially opened, the doctors in the camp treated several cases of heat exhaustion.[17]

The first patients to make use of the hospital facilities were a Union veteran from Philadelphia who needed help on June 26 and later the same day, a Confederate veteran from Hagerstown, Md., made his way to the hospital tent.

"These gentlemen quickly catching the spirit of the occasion, became friends, ate, slept, and dined together with the true campfire spirit," according to the Pennsylvania Reunion Commission Report.[19]

The first serious need for medical services in camp came on Monday, June 30.

Having received his cot, one veteran sets off to find his tent. *(Courtesy of the Library of Congress)*

ical men in the government service. By day the hospital will be indicated by Red Cross flags and at night by green lanterns," reported the *Washington Post*.[22]

The Pennsylvania National Guard posted handbills around the camp that listed health precautions the veterans should take:

"Get as much sleep as possible and be regular about it.

"Adhere in your diet to the rations furnished by the regular army, which are ample in quantity, excellent in quality, and sufficiently varied to gratify and satisfy all tastes.

"Don't indulge in intoxicating drinks. They disturb digestion and make you more susceptible to fatigue and disease.

"Take an extra pair of shoes with you, if possible. Nothing is more comfortable than a change of shoes and stockings. Tired feet are prevented in this way.

"Don't try to meet all the old comrades at once. The camp is a big one, but you have a week of it before you. Take it easy.

"In short, remember none of us is as young as we were fifty years ago, when we marched over the fields and hills of Gettysburg in '63."[23]

Not that you could convince some of the veterans who attended the reunion of that last fact. They were senior citizens, though they didn't act like it. One veteran was walking through Gettysburg and asked for directions back to the camp. He was told not to attempt to walk the distance because of the heat.

The veteran just shrugged and asked, "Why not? I walked all the way around Big Round Top and the Confederate line since breakfast and I guess I can go it to camp without getting any more tired. I watched for the shady places and I am feeling fine."[24]

Temperatures were dangerously high, par-

Gen. Daniel Sickles sits with some of his admirers near where he lost his leg during the Battle of Gettysburg. *(Courtesy of the Library of Congress.)*

Arriving veterans march into the Great Camp in preparation for the 50th reunion. (*Courtesy of the Library of Congress*)

ticularly since the veterans had little relief from high temperatures. The heat had baked the earth.

"'I never experienced anything like it before," said Charles Collins of Corfu, N.Y., who returned to Batavia July 3 with several other Genesee County veterans. "Why, at midnight on Tuesday the mercury registered at 100 degrees and at noon Tuesday it was 116 degrees in the shade. When we saw men falling over on every side it looked like the old battle days and we concluded it was time for us to leave."[25]

The camp's hospital and first-aid facilities were ready to hopefully handle any emergency that arose. The *New York Times* noted that the camp was well prepared "even with facilities to perform an appendicitis operation half an hour after diagnosis." The hospital sites were organized so that if a person fell sick or was hurt, they would be taken to a regimental hospital first and more serious cases would then be transported to a field hospital. The Red Cross supplied personnel to staff the 14 aid stations.

The elderly men hiked into the camp, though some succumbed to the heat. The men seemed ashamed that the heat could stop them. "It's hot," one veteran said, "but it isn't as hot as it was 50 years ago."[26]

Union and Confederate veterans would link arms and walk down the street in a show of unity.

"They marched the dusty road together from the village, they sat down at the

As the elderly veterans streamed off the many trains that arrived in Gettysburg (below) during the reunion, they were aided by Boy Scouts and soldiers who could get them to transportation. If the veteran had forgotten where he was staying or confused, each veteran had filled out an identification tags (above) that was carried at all times during the reunion. (*Courtesy of the Adams County Historical Society, Gettysburg, PA, and Library of Congress*)

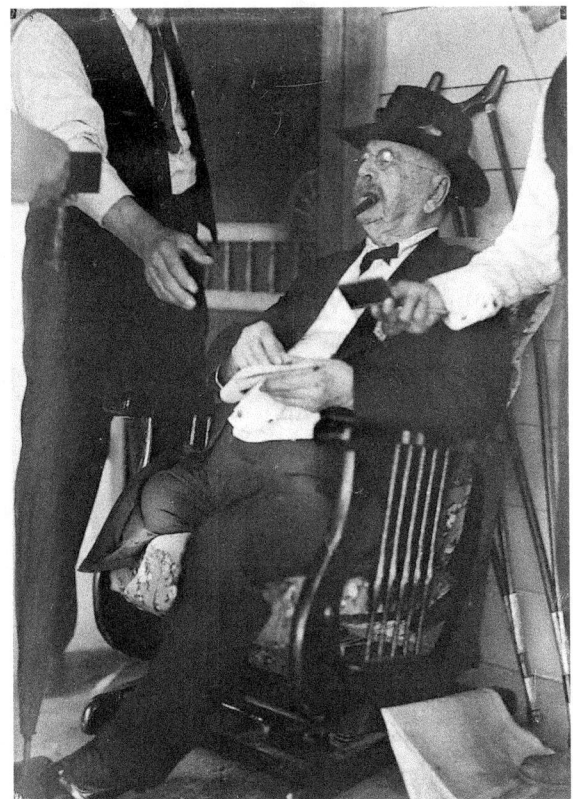

Gen. Daniel Sickles at the Gettysburg reunion. (*Courtesy of the Library of Congress*)

same mess tables, and they talked over the war before the same camp fires tonight. If there was any rancor in any heart any feeling of bitterness it did not come to the surface, and over the broad expanse of the "city" reunions of those who won and those who tried went on hour after hour."[27]

## SPECIAL ARRIVALS

Some of the special guests arrived early as well, including the governor of Virginia. He and his contingent drove to Gettysburg from the state that had once been the jewel of the Confederacy. Despite the heat, the Virginia veterans turned out along Emmitsburg Road to welcome their governor.

"While the men in gray stood waiting in the blazing sun for the Virginia governor to pass more than 100 automobiles filled with sightseers scurried over the road in front of them. Every man, bus as he might have been before he reached the straggling column lifted his hat and kept it off until he passed the end of the line."[28]

Another special guest to attend was General Daniel Sickles, the last surviving Union Corps commander from the Battle of Gettysburg. The 93-year-old veteran arrived late Sunday afternoon. He was accompanied by his housekeeper, Eleanor Wilmerding. He met the Rev. Dr. Joseph H. Twichell of Hartford, Conn., was the man who had given Sickles chloroform while his leg was amputated in 1863. Then, escorted by a troop of U.S. Regulars, Sickles went to the Rogers House where he sat on the porch and looked out over where he fell after a cannonball shattered his leg. From his position, he could see a stone monument that marked the spot.[29]

The people who were caring for the general during his stay at the reunion estimated that he must have shaken 3,000 hands while meeting his admirers at the Rogers' House.[30]

"Before the Southerners left the Rogers House they shouldered the general, carried

Gen. Daniel Sickles arrives in Gettysburg and is greeted by a large crowd of admirers. (*Courtesy of the Library of Congress*)

him out onto the battlefield, and stood him up before the camera fire and moving picture machines."[31]

As could be expected, Sickles waxed a bit nostalgic upon returning to the site where he had found fame and lost a leg.

"The wheat field looks the same today as it did 50 years ago. This occasion brings me to the height of my glory, and if the loss of my leg helped toward the cause of the nation, I am heartily glad. This is the best day of my life since that battle," Sickles said. "There have been times when I felt like it, but today I am a boy again., as young as you, young man, and this occasion will make me live to be 100."[32]

Helen D. Longstreet, widow of General James Longstreet was given two tents to use in the camp during the reunion. This was a special honor since the camp had been reserved for veterans and staff only.

## CONTINUING ARRIVALS

Elderly men continued arriving throughout Sunday. "All day long the trains poured their hundreds into the camp and by night-fall the number estimated under canvas was 18,000. To-day this was swollen to about 32,000, with more coming in every hour," the *Gettysburg Times* reported.[34]

Because of the heavy volume of traffic on the rail lines, the trains approached the region slowly in order to avoid any accidents. This caused many of the trains to arrive much later than originally planned.[35]

From midnight Sunday until noon Monday, 53 trains arrived in camp, each carrying between 200 and 500 veterans.[36] Many of these trains were direct specials and some even had cots on which the veterans could sleep during the journey and doctors who looked after them along the way.

## Recollections

When James H. Lansberry of St. Louis, Missouri, was in Gettysburg in 1863, he was a member of the 3rd Indiana Cavalry. He was captured during the battle and "detailed to assist in carry a wounded officer to the old seminary in Gettysburg. While in town frantic women flocked about him and begged that he tell of the battle. He remained to tell the story, with the result that he had to spend several days in following the Confederate army as a prisoner. After tramping 50 miles over rough country without shoes he succeeded in escaping and finally made his way back to Gettysburg, where he remained till August in assisting in the care of the wounded, where were housed in the seminary, churches, barns and public buildings."[33]

So many veterans arrived during the first day that it caught the U.S. Army officials in charge of the camp off guard. Veterans eventually made their way to the camp from the railroad stations only to find that there was no place for them to sleep. Some found space in the tents of their friends. Others slept outside during the warm night.

The next morning an emergency shipment of 25,000 additional blankets (each veteran was issued two) was ordered. Additional cots were also ordered and added to the existing tents so that they slept 10 veterans instead of eight.[37]

A special platform had been built in the camp so that veterans' trains could go directly there. Boy Scouts and soldiers met each arriving train. They would carry the veterans' luggage and give them directions to their state areas in the Great Camp. If the veteran looked exhausted or ill, he would be taken to a special tent where he could be examined and either taken by ambulance to a first aid station or his tent.

"Long streams of veterans could be seen wending their way about the streets hunting the camps of their particular states and from the dawn of the day until long after dark this line kept up," reported the *Gettysburg Times*.[38]

Veterans continued arriving, more and more by the hour.

"We expected 6,000 today, but we found tonight that we had about 25,000 to feed," said Col. Schoonmaker about the first day the Great Camp opened. "Although we were not looking for such a number, we were able to give every veteran something to eat before we went to bed. Tomorrow we will better handle the situation, and every man will get full rations."[39]

With such a large response, the kitchens weren't equipped to handle feeding everyone. They spread the available food around. Few of the veterans complained about the lack of provisions. They had all gotten by on less before, and for some of them, that time of skimpy rations had been 50 years earlier at Gettysburg.

"Two meals a day is good enough," said one veteran tonight, "that's more than we got 50 years ago."[40]

One might think that old men arriving in Gettysburg after a long journey would be exhausted and contemplative being back in a place where many of them had nearly died. Such was not the case.

> "Many of the veterans came into the encampment like a lot of boys out for a picnic. Laughing and chatting as they found their tents, calling and slapping each other on the back they frolicked about until they became weary and then sat down to talk over incidents of the war."[43]

Despite the heavy demand on Gettysburg's infrastructure and resources, the reunion was coming together nicely with minimal problems.

> "Every foot of the soil at Gettysburg is hallowed ground, made so by the blood

Dinner hour at the Great Camp and veterans line up at one of the kitchens to get their meal. *(Courtesy of the Library of Congress)*

# The Boy Scouts' Good Deeds

Hundreds of Boy Scouts came from cities like Philadelphia, Pa.; Washington D.C.; Burlington, N.J. and Hagerstown, Md., to help at the Grand Reunion. Seventy-five scouts came from Frederick, Md., with the Red Cross to assist where needed. Others came from as far away as 150 miles. The scouts guarded stores of supplies, ran errands and carried water for the veterans. They also patrolled the camp looking for people who might need assistance.

One official noted, "The manner in which they put up the tents assigned to their use when they reported for duty would have done credit to many military organizations that I have seen."[41]

Another encampment of 30 Boy Scouts on the Chambersburg-Gettysburg Pike near Cashtown, Pa., acted as traveler guides for visitors.[42]

*(photos courtesy of the Library of Congress and scanned from the Pennsylvania Reunion Commission Report)*

of fallen heroes. While the present celebration will take account of this, it will be no gloomy gathering. The only tears will be those of joy, and the catch in the throat will be the half-checked sob that contains no note of gathering of brothers all, and chant a song of gladness."[44]

## THE VETERANS

The arriving veterans ranged in age from 61

Veterans arriving in Gettysburg on one of the train specials. *(Courtesy of CivilWarBadges.com)*

unappeased regret. The thin blood of the old 'boys' will be stirred to quickstep action by memories of that earlier day. Thoughts of their valiant leaders and brave comrades already 'under the sod and the dew' will quiet the pulse again. And the choir invisible will look down from the celestial battlements upon a scene of peace, upon a to 112 years old. Micyah Weiss was the oldest veteran in attendance. He walked using two canes. His daughter drove him to the reunion from New York, but as the camp was for veterans and staff only, he went on alone from the camp gate and had no troubles getting around among his comrades.

John Lincoln Clem was the youngest veteran in attendance and he still served as a colonel in the Army. However when he had only been 10 years old, he ran away from home and joined General U.S. Grant's Army at Shiloh as a drummer boy.

All of the arriving veterans showed their pride in the cause they had served whether it had been Union or Confederate and there was no animosity towards those veterans from the opposing side. When John McClellan, a Confederate veteran who served on the ironclad *Merrimac*, came to Gettysburg, he didn't have a uniform to wear. McClellan was also a Crimean War veteran and would have been a veteran of the Spanish-American War, but he had been turned away because of his age. To show their support of McClellan and appreciation for his service, the Gettysburg Grand Army of the Republic post collected money and bought McClellan a Confederate uniform.

Another veteran, J.G. Wilson, of Dallas, Texas, had been a private in Company K, of the 12th Massachusetts during the Civil War. He fought in every principal battle during the war from Bull Run to Appomattox. After his tour of the battlefield, he walked to Spangler's Spring where he got down on his knees and sipped the cold water just as he had 50 years earlier on July 2, 1863, when he "almost dead from hunger and thirst."[45]

"It's great to get back here and to look over this old field again, which was strewn with blood when last I saw it, and it's great to see the old fellows who were kids when I knew them last," Wilson told a reporter. "I am going to have a good time here, and I am going to reassemble as many of my old comrades as possible to celebrate the various features of that battle in which we participated. They might build monuments on the old battlefield and otherwise beautify, but it's the same old place and brings back bloody, yet fond, reminiscences."[46]

One of the many photographers at work during the reunion saw a Confederate veteran

Some Civil War nurses attended the Grand Reunion. Pictured are Clarissa Dye, Cornelia Hanwik, Salome Stewart and Mary Stevens. (*Courtesy of the Library of Congress*)

and Union veteran talking near a cannon. He approached them and asked them to shake hands over the cannon while the photographer snapped a picture. The veterans agreed.

While holding hands over the cannon, the Union veteran said, "I'm mighty glad to do this, you know; but still, you know, we did lick you like hell."[47]

One group of Confederate soldiers got up before dawn and marched off to look for where their regiments had charged Cemetery Ridge. When they found it, they let loose with a Rebel Yell that woke some of still-sleeping veterans in the camp. Precautions had been taken to allow the veterans to get a good night's sleep each night to the extent that cars were not driven through the camp at night for fear the engine noise would wake the veterans so the sound of the Rebel Yell was certainly a shock.

silent nod to Pickett sent them down the ridge and across the valley of death and sang their war song to the sleeping camp of the Union soldiers. They ended it as they had begun, with that 'rebel yell' which had rung out as they marched down the ridge and up the elevation where the rain of fire began to pour down upon them from the mass of guns on Cemetery Ridge."[48]

A pair of veterans look for where they had been during the Battle of Gettysburg, *(Courtesy of the Library of Congress)*

Following the success of their scouting mission, the Confederate veterans returned to the Great Camp and went back to bed. When they woke a few hours later, they were ready to scout out other locations where they had fought.

The *New York Times* noted all the veterans' enthusiasm, "Their eager zest with which the old soldiers of both armies entered upon this task was almost boyish. They seem to be enjoying themselves as never before. Apparently, there never was a great crowd of which the mood was so uniform. It is a mood compounded of eager enthusiasm and happy excitement."[54]

One former Confederate soldier stood at the train station watching a group of Union veterans disembark from a train began laughing.

A veteran wearing his Union coat asked, "Well, what's so funny?"

"What in the dickens is that?" asked the startled Federals and the awakened regulars, digging sleep out of their eyes and peering out of their tent flaps, and then from far away across the battlefield came the voices of Pickett's men singing 'Dixie' from Seminary Ridge. There they stood in the gray of the coming dawn at the place where Longstreet's

Gettysburg College in 1913. *(Courtesy of the Library of Congress)*

# Gettysburg College and the Lutheran Theological Seminary

Gettysburg College and the Lutheran Theological Seminary were used to house specially invited guests to the reunion, such a politicians and high-ranking military officers. Between the two locations, 527 special guests were housed.[49]

"Old Dorm and South College resembled old-time castles being besieged, surrounded as they were by a multitude of tents," according to the Gettysburg College yearbook.[50]

The Pennsylvania State Police contingent assigned to the Grand Reunion camped out in tents on the college athletic fields. A large dining room tent was set up between "Old Dorm" and the gymnasium. Waiters served the guests their meals when they arrived.

> "The morning salutations as they made their way to the dining-room were: 'Good morning, General,' 'I trust you rested well, Major,' or 'The top of the morning to you, Governor.' Everybody had a title, but their bearing did not show it. They seemed more like a bunch of the 'old bodys' back for a class reunion."[51]

Like the Great Camp, military bands conducted evening concerts to the delight of the guests. Also, 60 automobiles were kept on hand to transport the guests at college to wherever they needed to go during the reunion.[52]

> "Out over the field there was, from dawn to sunset a line of vehicles taking tourists over the historic grounds. All day long, the avenues were dotted by the old worn men who had come back and were now trudging with a renewed strength over the ground which was stained by their own blood."[53]

These accommodations received high marks from the guests at the end of the reunion.

Shots from the Gettysburg College encampment for some of the special guests at the Grand Reunion. *(Courtesy of the Adams County Historical Society, Gettysburg, PA)*

A veteran takes a moment to write a letter home about the Gettysburg reunion.
*(Courtesy of the Library of Congress)*

"Funny! Why, it's the best joke in fifty years! In those days if we-all had told you-all that you'd be wearing gray, ye'd have shot us dead. Now, look at 'em. Every one of 'em all a-wearin' gray—gray of the Confederate States of America, sah, wearin' it 'cause God Almighty makes 'em wear it. Wearin' it in their hair and in their beards. Every last one of 'em a-wearing' the gray. Yes, sah, best joke in fifty years."[55]

The Rebel Gray uniform was almost as popular in the Great Camp as the Union Blue.

"Any man who wears it is sure of a tumultuous greeting from all the old men in blue who can get within gunshot of him. All through the streets to-day the same picture was being repeated every moment—some old man in gray coming along and being instantly pounced upon by half a dozen men in blue and being borne off in triumph. It is a real reunion, the genuine article."[56]

Further inside the camp, one Union veteran found his tent and quickly deposited his valise, hat, coat and vest. Then he walked off in search of some of his former comrades. Several hours later, he stopped at the information tent in the camp.

"Where in hell's tent 15? Or maybe it was 17?" the veteran asked the soldier manning the tent.

"But what avenue, sir? And what street?" the soldier asked.

"Avenue? Street? Plague if I know. Never mind."

The Union veteran was about to wander off again but the soldier stopped him and eventually guided the veteran back to his tent. The unfortunate man would be lost several more times during the reunion.[57]

The Grand Reunion was not a meeting of former enemies. These men were old friends. The presence of fellow soldiers who had lived through the same horrors reminded them of the gift of long life that they were all enjoying. It seemed to invigorate them. As one writer put it:

"Many were missing arms and legs. But no matter how trying their journeys, when they came among the other veterans all seemed to straighten a bit and walk with that elusive 'something' that always has characterized the American soldier."[58]

However, the soldiers were seniors and perhaps more prone to lose things than younger men. The camp's lost and found soon began filling with clothing, umbrellas, crutches, false teeth, and glasses "A discarded wooden leg never was claimed by its owner. One veteran, puzzling over a dozen sets of false teeth, suggested he try them all."[59]

The Great Camp itself was designed to provide as much comfort to the veterans as possible. A temporary post office was established inside the camp to handle incoming and outgoing mail during the reunion and telephones were wired into the camp so that one was never more than 400 feet away.[60]

Pennsylvania State Police augmented the soldiers and Boy Scouts to provide security in the camp and extra firefighting equipment was brought into Gettysburg in case a fire broke out in camp.[61]

The 8th Regimental Band from Carlisle, Pa., also stayed in the camp to provide concerts for the veterans in the camp each evening.

The scouts and soldiers regularly cleaned up the trash in the camp to keep it looking clean. D.W. Griffis of Batavia said, "There was nothing that even approached an odor. Empty cans were burned, every place was disinfected daily, garbage cans were removed before they were half filled. There was no litter and scarcely a fly was to be seen anywhere."[62]

Outside of their accommodations, perhaps the most-important thing that brought comfort to the veterans was plenty of food. The camp had multiple kitchens with dozens of bakers and cooks to prepare meals.

Griffis said, "I saw loaves of bread heaped as high as houses," he said. "We had chicken on the Fourth of July and everybody got all he could eat."[63]

Some of the menu items during the reunion included bacon and eggs for breakfast along with fried chicken, roast pork sandwiches, potatoes, gravy, vegetables, ice cream and Georgia watermelon for dinner.

Even outside of the camp, additional food stores were brought in. The Eagle Hotel arranged to have 3,600 eggs delivered daily. Another inn in Gettysburg bought 2,500 pounds of ham for the reunion business. In addition, hundreds of chickens were purchased to feed visitors.[64]

The inns and taverns in town had stocked up on plenty of beer and liquor expecting that the veterans would enjoy adult beverages with their refreshments. However, Lieutenant Colonel Alfred E. Bradley who had charge of the Army Field Hospital Service worried that the liquor would dehydrate the veterans or cause other health problems. He began asking that liquor not be sold during the time of the reunion.

With everything in place and the veterans arriving, the greatest military reunion in history was ready to begin.

> "To-day, on that same field, is being written an answer to the inspired and lofty thought of Lincoln such as even he, with all his profound love and intuitive understanding of this country, could hardly have foreseen. ... To the everlasting honor of these veterans may it always be gratefully remembered that they who had most cause not to forgive have ever been the most magnanimous in forgiving. They stand for the true spirit of American manhood, ad their patriotic example must be a noble inspiration for the youth of the present and all the generations to come."[65]

## THE GIRLS OF '63

On the evening before the official anniversary events began, many of the veterans gathered to honor someone other than the veterans.

On June 30, 1863, Union General John Buford had entered Gettysburg in pursuit of the Confederate army. According to the *New York Times*, "Gettysburg had been in a panic all day over the appearance of the Confederates, and its joy at seeing Buford's cavalrymen in their blue uniforms knew no bounds. As the cavalrymen rode through the streets they passed through lanes of Gettysburg girls in white dresses, who sang patriotic songs all the way and strewed flowers before them."⁶⁶

Captain Thomas Adams of the 6ᵗʰ New York Cavalry remembered it this way:

"As we came into the town we found on each side of the street rows of little girls, all dressed in white and singing 'John Brown's Body.' We were surprised and delighted, but we thought that was the end of it. A couple of blocks further on, however, we found another line, this time of young ladies of from 12 to 20, standing on dry goods boxes, grocery boxes, or anything else that could be hastily placed on the sidewalks to make a sort of platform. And so it went, as we rode through Gettysburg.

"What did they sing? Oh, patriotic songs. One of them, I remember, I had never heard before, but most of them were well known, such as 'Rally

Veterans march into the Great Camp from Gettysburg. *(Courtesy of the Library of Congress)*

Round the Flag.' It made a big impression on us, I can tell you, for we had come from Virginia, where we were not used to being received in that way. It was a mighty cheering preparation for the fight of the next day."⁶⁷

That sight and that welcome were not forgotten by the Union soldiers. When members of the 6ᵗʰ New York Cavalry heard about the 50ᵗʰ anniversary reunion in Gettysburg, they had started thinking about those young women who had welcomed them to the town in 1863 and wondering whether any of them were still in the area. When they reached Gettysburg, they scoured the town looking for the girls, now older women, who had greeted them 50 years earlier. They sent a car to collect any of the women they could find on June 30.

At 4 p.m., a few hundred veterans gathered under the Great Tent, which was large enough to hold 10,000 to 15,000 people. "A number of young cavalrymen of the regular army had come in to see what these old cavalrymen looked like, and everywhere could be seen some bent old man surrounded by three or four husky young fellows in khaki asking him eagerly all sorts of questions about what cavalry work was like in '63," according to the *New York Times*.⁶⁸

The women who had been part of the crowd that greeted Buford's men in 1863 and were still in Gettysburg fifty years later were: Mrs. Salome N. Steward who wore an American flag at her waist, Mrs. Sally Hearns, Mrs. Rupp, Miss Carrie Young, Mrs. Sheads and Mrs. William Tawney. They were all escorted to the grandstand while the band played a march.

Major Jerome B. Wheeler of the 6ᵗʰ New York Cavalry said to them, "If absence makes the heart grow fonder, how our hearts go out to you to-day as we look into your dear faces after an absence of fifty years. We left you most sorrowfully and regretfully, and we now come to you from all parts of the country to tender our regret that our first visit was so brief and our years of absence so inevitable. And we to thank you and say, 'God Bless You' for the friendly greeting you extended to us in those days so long ago, when kind words from gentle and noble women were like an oasis in a desert."⁶⁹

The soldiers then called on the women to sing one of the songs they had sung fifty years previously.

Steward told them, "We don't think we can sing so well as we did fifty years ago."

The veterans weren't looking for excellent singing, though, they were looking for memories.

"We want singers!" shouted the cavalrymen. "It's the singers we want!"

The band began playing "Rally Round the Flag." It was interrupted frequently by cheers from the veterans. When the song finished, the crowd shouted "Hurrah for the girls of '63!"

Then, without any accompaniment, the women began singing the same song that the men of Buford's Cavalry had heard when they had ridden into Gettysburg fifty year ago.

"Whether the voices were or were not so good as they were fifty years ago, they sounded clear and sweet in the big tent, and no grand opera singer ever had such an appreciative audience. The old men listened as if they were hearing Melba. Many of them were wiping their eyes."⁷⁰

The *New York Times* reported that the men were so entranced by the singing that when one soldier turned to say something to another, "it looked as if he would be lynched for the sacrilege. He was silenced as if he had committed a crime, and was hustled to the back of the crowd by indignant hands."⁷¹

When the ladies finished, the band struck up another song that everyone in the tent joined in singing. At the end of the song, a Confederate veteran in the crowd let loose with a Rebel Yell that surprised those in attendance, but was then joined with cheers and applause.

A group of Indiana veterans gather outside of their tent in the Great Camp. *(Courtesy of the Library of Congress)*

Afterwards, soldiers began calling out to the women.

One man climbed onto the grandstand and approached Sheads, "Were you one of the girls that stood on the soapbox nearest the corner on the first street as you come down from the Cashtown Road?"

Another veteran said, "I was a member of the 8th Illinois Cavalry. I shall never forget the reception these ladies gave us, and I wish to thank them for it. I've at a home a limp, purple ribbon given me by girl about 10 years old as we came through the streets. This young lady stepped out from the sidewalk and tried to pin a bouquet on me. She was too little to reach up so far, so I got off my horse and she pinned the bouquet on and gave me this purple ribbon and said: 'Soldier, I want you to wear this ribbon in the next fight you're in, the one you're going to have now.' I said: 'Thank you, my little lady, and I will, if there is a fight, but I don't think we will have one.' She said: 'Oh, yes, you will, soldier. There's thousands of rebels here, and you will surely have a fight.' I said: 'I hope not, but I thank you very much, and if there is a fight I will wear it.' I did wear it, and I've kept it ever since. It's at my home in Aurora, Ill. I wish I could see that young lady."

This memory caused a bit of contention when a gray-bearded Union veteran stood up and said, "The 8th Illinois Cavalry did not open the battle of Gettysburg. Back home I am known as the fighting Quaker of Conshohocken or the Hero of Gettysburg, and I want it thoroughly understood that the Pennsylvania Cavalry opened the battle."

The Illinois veteran was going to argue the point when a New York veteran spoke up and said that the 6th New York had opened the battle.

Wheeler shouted over the crowd, "There is no man on God's footstool who knows who opened the battle."

His plea had no effect and veterans began shouting to defend their position as the men had started the Battle of Gettysburg. Finally, Steward stood up and indicated to the noisy crowd that she wanted to say something. She achieved with a soft voice what Wheeler couldn't with his shouts. The crowd fell silent.

"I have often been asked how we came to sing," she began. "I will tell you. There was nothing pre-concerted. On the Friday before the battle a part of the rebel army occupied Gettysburg. They left on Saturday morning and on Saturday afternoon and Sunday we were nearly crazy. We didn't know who was coming-whether it was the Union soldiers or the Confederates. And when we saw Buford's cavalry coming we were so delighted, the revulsion of feeling was so delighted, the revulsion of feeling was so great that we just had to do something. Somebody said, 'Let's sing as they come in,' and it went over the town like wildfire."

Boys Scouts rough-housing during their free time at the Grand Reunion. *(Courtesy of the Adams County Historical Society, Gettysburg, PA)*

The situation diffused, the men of Buford's Cavalry all went up to have their turn at shaking hands with the women who had cheered them up fifty years ago.

Veterans resting after a hard day of sightseeing. *(Courtesy of the Library of Congress)*

Rupp beckoned to a Confederate veteran in the crowd who walked over to her.

"I see you are a Confederate, and I wanted to tell you that we had something to do with the Confederate Army, as well as with the Union soldiers, fifty years ago, so that we feel as if we know you as well as we do them. I was one of the girls who carried water to the wounded Confederates of Archer's Brigade," Rupp told the man.

Then Steward chimed in, "Our house was used as a Union and Confederate hospital alike. We girls went about town at night, when the Confederate and Union soldiers occupied the town, and we never heard a disrespectful word from a soldier of either army."[72]

Once again, these women led the way showing that though they might have been Confederate and Union, they were all Americans.

# 4

# Veterans' Day
# July 1, 1913

"Veterans' Day" was the theme of the first official day of the Grand Reunion. It was a time for the veterans to renew old acquaintances. Men from 46 of the 48 states tramped over the battlefield reliving horrifying memories and appreciating the fact that they were still alive 50 years later. Though the fields and hills looked familiar, hundreds of monuments now marked the sites where various actions had taken place in 1863.

Despite the tens of thousands veterans in attendance, the former soldiers were more likely to notice the high number of friends and comrades who were missing from their ranks and how frail those who were in attendance appeared.

Looks can be deceiving, though.

Groups of veterans woke in the morning, ate a filling breakfast in one of the mess tents and started off on their various sightseeing tours.

One group of Confederate veterans spent the morning hiking from the Great Camp to the Peach Orchard and then to the Wheat Field, Devil's Den and up the slope to Little Round Top. Their last stop of the morning was at the Angle, the site of Pickett's Last Charge. They walked back to the camp for "a bit of liquid comfort" and then hiked into Gettysburg and back.

The total distance covered by these senior citizen veterans was about eighteen miles,[1] a distance that would be daunting to many much younger men today.

## VETERAN ADVENTURES

Though many veterans had been in Gettysburg for days, the formal opening of the reunion was not until July 1, the anniversary of the beginning of the battle in 1863. The *New York Times* noted that it was only the opening event not the keystone one. "The event was the hunting up of the man who shot you, if you could find him, and if you couldn't, then the hunting up of the man whose regiment fought yours. There was an amazing number of such reunions," according to the newspaper.²

Many such meetings were taking place in camp, on the battlefield and in town.

One Virginia veteran arrived late in the camp and went looking for his tent. He walked from tent to tent, opening the flap and asking any veterans inside where he could find his regiment. Finally, the lost Johnny Reb wandered into the area where survivors of the 1st Minnesota Regiment, which had suffered 82 percent casualties at Gettysburg, were staying. At the fifth tent he came to, he explained his problem to the veteran inside and was asked to what regiment the Minnesotan had belonged.

Showing that any past animosity was forgotten, the group welcomed their former enemy into the tents. They sat around out of the hot sun talking and reminiscing over liquor.

"And who were you with, Johnnie?" one Minnesotan asked.

"Twenty-eighth Virginia," the former Confederate replied.

"That would be Olmstead's men?"

"Right. And we met you 1st Minnesota fellows off yonder—there where the lightning was thickest."

"Well, I'll be damned."

Then one of the Minnesotans asked, "Say, do you know what became of the 28th Virginia's flag that day up yonder?"

A young Boy Scout poses for a picture with some of the veterans at the reunion. (*Scanned from the Pennsylvania Commission Report*)

An aerial view of the Great Camp at Gettysburg. (*Courtesy of the Library of Congress*)

# FEEDING

According to the Pennsylvania Reunion Commission Report, 2,000 cooks and helpers in 173 kitchens with 425 army field ranges prepared the camp meals.

- Greatest number of meals prepared in a day: 168,000 on July 1.

- Total number of meals prepared: 688,000 from supper on June 29 to breakfast on July 6.

***The Grocery List***

| | |
|---|---|
| Meats | 156,410 lbs. |
| Fish | 7,008 cans |
| Poultry | 14,722 lbs. |
| Vegetables | |
|     Canned | 30,053 cans |
|     Dried | 17,795 lbs. |
|     Fresh | 216,777 lbs. |
| Macaroni | 3,500 lbs. |
| Butter | 12,383 lbs. |
| Eggs | 24,930 doz. |
| Dried Fruit | 22,500 lbs. |
| Cereals | 21,153 lbs. |
| Tea | 1,631 lbs. |
| Coffee | 12,206 lbs. |
| Sugar | 59,976 lbs. |
| Lemons | 85 boxes |
| Ice Cream | 2,015 gals. |
| Cakes | 53,000 doz. |
| Pies (2.5 lbs.) | 7,000 |
| Pepper | 500 lbs. |
| Vinegar | 400 gals. |
| Pickles | 403 gals. |
| Salt | 9,300 lbs. |
| Hard Bread | 10,000 lbs. |
| Flour | 130,048 lbs. |
| Also issued: | |
| Wood | 720 cords |

# AN ARMY

*Also Issued*
| | |
|---|---|
| Wood | 720 cords |
| Coal | 18,000 lbs. |
| Ice | 62,669 lbs. |
| Hay | 247,321 lbs. |
| Lumber | 216,676 ft. |

(Photos courtesy of the Library of Congress and Adams County Historical Society, Gettysburg, PA.)

"I don't," said the old Confederate. "You see, I was with Armistead's brigade, the one that got into the Yankee lines when Pickett made his charge and made what they call the 'high-water mark of the rebellion.' I don't rightly remember just what happened to the flag after we jumped into those Yankee batteries but I think some of you Yankees got it."

"We did," said the man in the tent. "I'm Capt. T. H. Pressnal of Company F, First Minnesota. We captured your flag, and we've got it now in St. Paul. The other fellows in this tent will be in in a minute, and all of them belonged to the regiment that got your flag. We've got a spare blanket here and you'll never find your tent to-night. Come in and bunk with us."

Since the night was getting darker, the Virginian accepted the offer. In the morning, he told his hosts, "You know, I've been a-lyin' here thinkin'. As long as some of you Yanks had to get that flag, I'm mighty glad it were you-all. You're right good people."[3]

Ward G. Wallace had served with the Confederate 7th Texas Regiment and Edward Cox had served with the 2nd New York Cavalry. They were in camp and about to pass each other when they stopped. They stared at each other and said, nearly in unison, "I know you!"

Cox pointed across the camp and said, "Do you see that very tree over there? Well, I saw you there on July 2, 1863."

"You're right," replied Wallace. "And now I know who you are. You're that fellow who was hit in the leg and couldn't run."

"Yes, Billy, I remember. I'm mighty glad I didn't shoot, for if I had this couldn't have happened."[4]

Battle of the bands, Civil War style. (*Courtesy of the Library of Congress*)

Out on the battlefield, a gray-bearded Confederate veteran of Pickett's Charge, A. C. Smith of Virginia told of his experience during the charge. He walked along Cemetery Ridge with other fellow Confederates. The other men deferred to him because he was one of the few survivors of Pickett's Charge.

Old enemies meet as friends at Gettysburg. (*Courtesy of the Library of Congress*)

"Well, here I was. And right here's where I leaped across. I got a yard beyond that wall, I reckon, when I got hit and down I went. I remember a chap in blue runnin' at me. He had a bayonet, and I thought I was a goner. But he give me a drink of water from his canteen. And then blamed if he didn't pick me up and carry me off to a Yank hospital.

"I never saw him again. I reckon he's gone to his reward by this time," Smith told the veterans in his group.

Another group of veterans was nearby listening to a Union veteran tell about his experience. R. N. Hamilton, stood with his hands clasped behind his back studying the battlefield. He told his audience, "The Rebs got to about here. Then we beat 'em back. And it was right here..." Hamilton pointed to the wall. "...that a Johnny fell into my arms. I lifted him up and gave him a swig from my canteen. Then I got him on my shoulders and carried him off."

Smith heard Hamilton and drew closer to get a good look at the man. Suddenly, he interrupted Hamilton and shouted, "Well, Praise the Lord; Praise the Lord it's you, brother."

The two men embraced and Hamilton said, "Fifty years ago. Don't that beat all!"[5]

Some reunions didn't end so happily. One former Union soldier in his faded blue uniform found the person he was looking for in the Soldiers' National Cemetery beneath a small tombstone that read "William Henry Scott."

He held his cap in his hand as tears rolled down his cheeks.

"After the first day's fighting, they carried me into a hospital, badly wounded," the soldier

Two veterans re-enact a battle using their canes for rifles. (*Scanned from the Pennsylvania Commission Report*)

# Wedding Bells

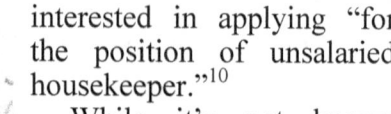

Though most of the Civil War veterans returned to Gettysburg to meet up with old war buddies, a few came looking for love. A resident of St. James, Mo. wrote to Gettysburg Burgess J. A. Holtzworth in late May 1913. He noted that he and a group of four or five other Missouri veterans were coming to the reunion. They were hoping that the burgess could direct them toward some single women.

The Missourian wrote, "...if you have got a few good widows or old maids who would like to marry and go west, we can accommodate a few. They must be good housekeepers and not too young."

The *Gettysburg Times* noted that the burgess would forward the names and contact information of any women who were interested in applying "for the position of unsalaried housekeeper."[10]

While it's not known whether any of the Missourians got married, at least one veteran did. James Goodwin of New York met Margaret Murphy of Chicago in Gettysburg and the two of them were wed. They had been engaged 46 years previously, but something had happened and the marriage was called off. Both Goodwin and Murphy wound up marrying others. After Goodwin became a widower and Murphy a widow, they reconnected and decided to marry once again, which they did when Goodwin came to Gettysburg for the reunion.[11]

Veterans relax near the bakery wood piles in the Great Camp. *(Courtesy of the Adams County Historical Society, Gettysburg, PA)*

said to his companions. "Next to me was a young Southerner, from Georgia. We two chummed up in the hospital ... and he told me his name was William Henry Scott. He told me of his plantation and I told him of my home in New York. We came to love each other ... promised when each got better that we'd come and visit one another ... I was sent home; he stayed behind to get well. But he never came to see me ..."

The man paused in his storytelling and shook his head. "Hoped to see him here. And here he is; here he is."[6]

Throughout the camp the Union and Confederacy were meeting once again, but rather than trying to best each other in battle, they were trying to best each other with boasts.

One former Confederate cavalryman said, "I tell you, friends, there weren't no more smarter troops than old Jeb Stuart's. He taught you Yanks what cavalry was for."

A Union veteran countered with, "Well, Johnnie, the truth is we used to let Stuart's boys run through our lines just for the fun of seeing how fast they could ride."[7]

The temporary post office in the camp was doing a heavy business as veterans mailed off postcards to friends and family about the events of the reunion. The post office handled 75,000 pieces of mail on July 1.[8]

However, despite the tens of thousands of veterans in the camp and tramping across the battlefield, there wasn't much of a need for them to go into town and there weren't as many visitors as expected staying around the town. Estimates were that there were 4,000 people staying in Gettysburg when businesses had prepared for 15,000 to 20,000. Eighty percent of the homes in town had prepared to take in lodgers and many of them were empty.

> "Apparently discouraged and frightened by the stories which gained circulation through the public press of the country, that the town would not be able to feed the enormous crowds, that the railroads would have trouble bringing them here and getting them home after the anniversary, that there might be a food shortage and other adverse reports, many thousands have been deterred from coming here and financial losses are reported on all sides."[9]

## THE DAY'S EVENTS

The official events of the day began at 2 p.m. in the large tent that could seat between 10,000 to 15,000 people depending on how tightly they were packed in under the canvas.

After the opening music, Col. James M. Schoonmaker, a Civil War veteran and Medal of Honor winner, gave the opening remarks as

U.S. Secretary of War Lindley M. Garrison
*(Courtesy of the Library of Congress)*

chairman of the Pennsylvania Reunion Commission. He noted that these former enemies were now "assembled on this historic field over which they struggled, in closest friendly relationship, citizens of one country, with one flag, made a hundred fold stronger and more enduring by their mighty deeds on this and a hundred other battlefields."[12]

The Grand Army of the Republic Chaplain Reverend Dr. George E. Lovejoy gave the opening prayer. He noted, "We may well put off our shoes from our feet for the place whereon we stand is holy ground. Holy indeed, because of precious blood shed upon these slopes and in these vales."[13]

U.S. Secretary of War Lindley M. Garrison gave the first of the four addresses of the day. He told the gathered veterans that Gettysburg was once again the center of the world's attention. However, unlike as in 1863, those gathered together in 1913 were doing so in peace.

"Once again does this field tremble under the tread of a mighty host-not now in fear, however, but in joy. The field of enmity has become the field of amity. You have trodden under your feet the bitter weeds of hate and anger, and in their places

## Spam and Gettysburg

Though Spam canned ham wasn't officially introduced until 1937, a form of the canned, boneless meat was first introduced during the 50th reunion at Gettysburg.

"In order to handle the group, which far exceeded the original attendance estimates, an entirely new system of supply had to be improvised. During the encampment, selected cuts of fresh beef were chilled and boned in packing houses, and then packed in lined wooden shipping boxes," according to the U.S. Army Quartermaster Museum.[19]

The cases of canned meat were refrigerated and shipped on trains to Gettysburg where they were used in the camp kitchens to feed the veterans. The cooks would slice the meat into steaks that they would fry and broil for entrees.

"The importance of the Gettysburg experience went more or less unrecognized until shipping shortages in World War I forced Army subsistence personnel to look for new ways to try to conserve space onboard cargo ships going to Europe," according to the U.S. Army Quartermaster Museum.[20]

At that time, Lieutenant Jay C. Hormel of the U.S. Army Quartermaster Corps returned from France to develop a large-scale production system. With the success of the system, canned meat became a staple of army field rations beginning in World War I. Hormel's production and supply system eventually became SPAM and Hormel became president of the George A. Hormel and Hormel Company in Austin, Minn.[21]

have sprung up the pure flowers of friendship and love."[14]

Garrison told the veterans that the reunion was important because the memories created during the reunion would replace those of the battle. "It will no longer picture itself in your memories as a field of carnage and suffering and woe, but a field of smiling faces and happy hears and great joys," Garrison said.[15]

Pennsylvania Governor John Tener followed Garrison. He told the group that the point of the reunion wasn't to celebrate a victory but to show the world that North and South, Union and Confederate, were now united. This is what the veterans had gathered for and that because of their ability to put aside those differences, the country was able to grow greater.[16]

Following some interim music, Alfred Beers, commander-in-chief of the Grand Army of the Republic, and then Bennett H. Young, commander-in-chief of the United Confederate Veterans spoke before the assembled crowd.

"Here today Confederates appear in their uniforms with their war-torn banners, and the soldiers who wore the Blue are here with their uniforms; and the Flag of Our Country is floating over

A group of veterans set off on a sightseeing hike on the Gettysburg battlefield. *(Courtesy of the Adams County Historical Society, Gettysburg, PA)*

all, to declare that there is a complete and thorough and unqualified and unchangeable restoration of good faith and kindness. This occasion declares, when we come to consider our nation and future, that there is no North, no South, no East, no West, but simply a great Republic which finds in the spirit of its people patriotic pride, unchanging loyalty, and unfailing devotion to the highest principles of human liberty."[17]

To show the balance of the reunion, the Reverend Dr. H. M. Hammill, chaplain of the United Confederate Veterans closed the ceremony that that had been opened by the chaplain of the Grand Army of the Republic.

Following the opening ceremony, the veterans left the tent and headed for the mess tents and one of the filling meals that were prepared for them by the cooks and cook helpers supplied by the army.

"All the meals were excellent. Everyone had a choice of either steak, ham and eggs, beans, or hash for breakfast. Dinner was roast beef, lamb, or boiled corned beef with all the fixings, including pie or pudding. Cold meats, fried potatoes, and prunes made up the supper and always after we emptied the large tin coffee cup we could get it filled with ice cream."[18]

A pair of the regular army guards at Gettysburg who watched over the veterans during the Grand Reunion. *Courtesy of the Library of Congress)*

Veterans at the reunion pose for a picture on the battlefield. *(Courtesy of the Library of Congress)*

Feeding 54,000 veterans was similar to feeding an army. It took a lot of planning to be able to not only have enough food to feed them but to feed them in a timely manner. For instance, it had originally been considered to seat the veterans at tables, but when it was discovered that it would require 40 acres of space, long tables were settled upon. Also, 14 refrigerated rail cars were needed to store the meat and ice cream for the reunion.[22]

Following the meal, some of the veterans wandered back over the battlefield or retired to their tents. Before long, though, the veterans would gather in groups sitting outside their tents and enjoying the cool evening breezes. They would tell their stories of the battle and renew old relationships. According to John Haines of the Boston Lincoln Group, "You would join a group all in earnest conversation expecting to hear a story of the war and instead find they were debating some passage from the Bible; another time it would be current politics, but the most talked about subject was the wonderful time they were having there on this old battleground."[23]

However, the camp reunions weren't enough for some of the veterans. Some wandered into Gettysburg looking for some fun, but the saloons and bars in town closed at 10:30 p.m. It wasn't something that the saloon keepers wanted, but Col. Bradley had requested it as a way of trying to keep things from getting too rowdy among the 54,000 veterans who were reliving their glory days. Bradley had made the request of Gov. Tener who said he didn't have the authority. The Gettysburg city fathers didn't want to take responsibility for curtailing business in town and it finally fell on Burgess Anderson to decide.[24]

Other veterans simply decided to take a walk through the battlefield at night. Some of them got lost along the way and wound up taking a longer walk than they had planned. Two of these men were found the following morning walking along Long Lane and arguing, but not about the way.

> "I toll you that is the moon," said one. "Hurry, or we will lose our way when it grows darker."
>
> "I'll be you $10 it's not the moon, it the sun," said the other, and he produced his money. Thus they stood arguing until another comrade a little under the weather, came ambling along. He was called into consultation as to whether it was the sun or the moon.
>
> "'Deed, I couldn't tell you, boys," he apologized. "I haven't been in this place for 50 years."[25]

A modern soldier shows a Civil War veteran the tools of modern warfare. (*Courtesy of the Library of Congress*)

# 5

# MILITARY DAY
# JULY 2, 1913

The second day of the Grand Reunion was "Military Day" with speeches that focused on the importance of the U.S. military both during the Civil War and in the 20th Century.

Meanwhile, veterans were still continuing to arrive in Gettysburg for the reunion.

> "By every train day and night for the last six days the republic's scarred heroes have poured into this quaint, sleepy town in the hills of Pennsylvania, this tilt yard of American chivalry. The crippled legions who stood behind the guns on these Pennsylvania battle heights, the broken ranks who charged across the valleys, now white and peaceful under Summer suns, once more tread the streets of Gettysburg. In the gray dawns and purple twilights of these July days America listens as they march on, to the tramp, tramp of the Old Guard. The men who were at Gettysburg when the Peach Orchard was a field of blood and Cemetery Ridge was a peak of fire are at Gettysburg again, and for the last time perhaps."[1]

One of the arriving veterans was John B. Hawley. He had been a police sergeant at Fort Monroe in Virginia during the Civil War and one of Confederate President Jefferson Davis's guards while Davis was in prison. When Hawley heard about the reunion, he was determined to attend.

> "Fearing that his son, Charles B. Hawley, a director of the Northumberland Trust & Safe Deposit Company, would keep him from coming to Gettysburg to attend the fiftieth anniversary celebration, feeble John Hawley, 85 years old, a veteran of the Civil War, climbed out of a window and took the first train for the camp grounds."[2]

The veterans also continued meeting up with their former enemies and burying the hatchet, sometimes literally. The *Gettysburg Times* told the story of a Union veteran and a Confederate veteran who met in Gettysburg.

> "After a tour of the town they hit upon a great scheme. They walked hand in hand through the streets to a hardware store, bought a hatchet and tramped a mile and a half to the battlefield. They hunted up the Bloody Angle, dug a hole in the ground there, and, with embraces, buried the hatchet."[3]

Elsewhere in the Great Camp, Augustus J. Washburne of Philadelphia met the Confederate soldier who cut off his arm during the battle. It had happened during a hand-to-hand fight the two men had at the High Water Mark.

While touring the different places he had fought at during the battle, he eventually made it to the place where he had lost his arm to a Rebel bayonet. It was there that he happened to see the Confederate veteran who had wielded that bayonet. His name was James Burnett of Indianapolis, Ind.

Washburne walked over to the man and asked him if he remembered the incident and Burnett looked at him and shouted, "By gosh, you are the fellow!"

The two men became friends and within half an hour, the two men were calling each other "Jim" and "Gus."[4]

A similar meeting took place between Col. Schoonmaker and Orlando Douglass, a Confederate veteran at the reunion. Douglass walked up to Schoonmaker and said that the colonel probably didn't remember him, but that he remembered Schoonmaker because he had shot at Douglass during the battle and barely missed him. Douglass had been captured during the battle and put into a prison

Veterans recall the Battle of Gettysburg.
*(Courtesy of the Library of Congress)*

# The Gettysburg Cyclorama

One of the popular attractions at Gettysburg continues to be the Gettysburg Cyclorama, which houses the painting called "The Battle of Gettysburg" painted by French artist Paul Philippoteaux. The painting shows "Pickett's Charge," the climax of the Battle of Gettysburg. However, unlike most paintings, this one is a cylindrical painting that is 359 feet around and 27 feet tall. You can stand in the center of a room and almost feel as if you are in the middle of the battle.

Philippoteaux came to Gettysburg in April 1882 and spent several weeks studying the battlefield, making preliminary sketches, researching the battle and taking photographs. He even interviewed survivors of the battle to hear their stories. Then with five assistants, he spent a year and a half painting the battle. The finished work was nearly 100 yards long and weighed six tons.[9]

Four versions of the painting were actually done. The first was originally shown in Chicago, but was then lost for decades until it was rediscovered in 1965 and purchased by a group of North Carolina investors.

The second painting was originally shown in Boston. When it was replaced temporarily by another cyclorama painting in 1891, it was shown for a time in Philadelphia. However, when the Battle of Gettysburg returned to Boston it wasn't immediately put on display and was damaged while in storage.

Albert Hahne of Newark, N. J., purchased this damaged version in 1910. He displayed it in Newark; Baltimore, Md.; New York City, N. Y. and Washington D.C.

On September 3, 1912, ground was broken for a cyclorama building on Baltimore Street in Gettysburg near the entrance to Soldiers' National Cemetery. It was during the 50th battle reunion that the Gettysburg Cyclorama opened for the public.

The National Park Service purchased it in 1942 and moved it to a new location in Ziegler's Grove when the old visitor's cen-

Previous page: Left, Paul Philippoteaux painting the cyclorama. *(Courtesy of Wikimedia Commons)*

ter opened in 1961.

It remained there until 2005 when it was closed, underwent extensive renovation and moved to a new location within the new National Park Visitors' Center on Baltimore Street. Olin Conservation, the company that did the renovation, found some original pieces of the painting that had been thought lost and were able to add back an additional 12 feet of the painting and restore 14 vertical feet of sky. The new cyclorama opened in September 2008.

A third version of the painting that was originally shown in Philadelphia was destroyed and the fourth version, which was originally shown in Brooklyn, N.Y., is currently lost.

Above, a portion of the Gettysburg cyclorama. Right, the original building that housed the cyclorama. *(Photos courtesy of the Library of Congress)*

Above: Veterans reminiscing during the Gettysburg reunion. *(Courtesy of the U.S. Militaria Forum)* Left: A veteran takes a break to write a letter home *(Courtesy of the Library of Congress)*

under Schoonmaker's command. "The Colonel laughed and insisted upon hearing the whole story told over again," according to The *Gettysburg Times*.[5]

During the comments at the day's afternoon events, Dr. Nathaniel D. Cox told the audience, "Comrades and friends, these splendid statues of marble and granite and bronze shall finally crumble to dust, and in the ages to come, will perhaps be forgotten, but the spirit that has called this great assembly of our people together, on this field, shall live for ever."[6]

The temperature climbed to 102 degrees in the shade at the start of the afternoon's speeches, but with so many men crowded together under the canvas it probably went even higher. However, the heat was momentarily forgotten when General Bennett H. Young, commander in chief of the United Confederate Veterans, rose and bowed to him "I can give you something that no one else can give you. We will now give you the rebel yell."[7]

Nine Confederate generals and 1,000 men shouted out with a famous call that was heard throughout the camp.[8]

The beastly hot weather changed in the afternoon as heavy rains fell along with strong winds, loud thunder and violent lightning. The veterans took shelter in the camp tents and shared stories as the rain settled the dust on the roads and cleaned the canvas tents. While the rains kept the veterans under canvas and off the battlefield, they did enjoy the cooler temperatures that came with the rain.

Not all of the veterans were lucky enough to be near camp, though when the storm swept in and they were forced to find shelter where they could. "They huddled for shelter on the lee side of the big boulders of Devil's Den, while the lightning played around them, crashing into trees and streaking the sharp edges of the big stone piles with strange

Veterans sightseeing at Gettysburg. *(Courtesy of the Library of Congress)*

light," according to the *New York Times*.[10]

The storm lasted about an hour and afterward, the veterans then went back onto the battlefield. They were joined by boys and women hunting for bullets uncovered by the rain. "It seems that a harvest of bullets is always collected after a heavy storm has washed away some of the surface, and this is a recognized Gettysburg industry, reported the *New York Times*.[11]

Though North and South got along well during the reunion, each side still strongly supported the country for which they had fought. This led to an unpleasant incident in the Gettysburg Hotel on the evening of July 2.

"The fight started suddenly and was over in a few minutes. The dining room was full, and the disturbance caused a panic. The old veteran, who was unhurt and who disappeared in the melee, was sitting near Farbor and Carroll when he heard the slighting remarks about Lincoln. He jumped to his feet and began to defend the martyred President and to berate his detractors. The men who were stabbed jumped to the defense of the veteran when others closed in. Knives were out in a second. Women fled for the doors and crowded to the windows ready to jump to the street."[12]

In all, seven men were stabbed, though none died from their injuries. W. B. Henry of Philadelphia was arrested for causing the fight. He was not a veteran of Gettysburg himself, but his father was R.R. Henry of Tazwell, Virginia, who had served as a Confederate general during the war. The wounded men were: Edward J. Carroll, sergeant of the Quartermaster's Corps; David Farbor of Butler, Pa. and a member of the State Constabulary, John D. Maugin of Harrisburg; Malcolm Griffin of Bedford, Pa.; Charles Susler of West Fairview, Pa.; Hayden Renisbecker of Gettysburg and Harry A. Root, Jr. of Harrisburg.

The incident spurred the state Board of Health to request once again that all of the saloons and bars in Gettysburg be shut down for the duration of the reunion.

U.S. Army soldiers get a briefing on their job to patrol the Great Camp. *(Scanned from the Pennsylvania Reunion Commission report)*

NO NORTH, NO SOUTH...

Left: A souvenir medal given to veterans who attended the Gettysburg reunion. Above: Veteran musicians prepare to play a tune at Gettysburg. Below: Veterans at Devil's Den during the reunion. (*Scanned from the Pennsylvania Reunion Commission Report*)

## The First Gettysburg Movie

The first movie about Gettysburg, *The Battle of Gettysburg,* made its debut at Walter's Theatre on June 26, 1913, just as the first veterans were arriving for the Grand Reunion. It was a black-and-white silent film. Any prints of the movie have been lost to time, but according to *IMDB.com*, the 50-minute movie tells the story of a young woman's sweetheart who fights for the Union Army while her brother fights for the Confederate Army. They come face-to-face during the Battle of Gettysburg.

The movie stars Willard Mack and Charles K. French. Mack played Abraham Lincoln in the film. Charles Giblyn and Thomas H. Hince are credited as the directors.

Though considered a "lost" film, some of the battle footage can be seen in the comedy, *Cohen Saves the Flag.* The battle sequences were shot together in Malibu, California. Also, according to the web site, *The Silent Era*, a version of the film was screened in France in 1973.[13]

Veterans visit one of the monuments on the Gettysburg battlefield. *(Scanned from the Pennsylvania Reunion Commission report)*

# 6

# Civic Day
# July 3, 1913

The third day of the Grand Reunion was recognized by two themes. Some called it "Civic Day" and others called it "Governor's Day." The former wasn't too surprising seeing as how 11 governors spoke during the afternoon's formal event that also included speeches from Vice President Thomas R. Marshall and Speaker of the House of Representatives, Champ Clark.

The governors who spoke to the assembled veterans were:
- Simeon E. Baldwin of Connecticut
- James S. Cox of Ohio
- Adolph O. Eberhardt of Minnesota
- William T. Haines of Maine
- Louis B. Hanna of North Dakota
- William Hodges Mann of Virginia
- James McCreary of Kentucky
- Charles R. Miller of Delaware
- Samuel R. Ralston of Indiana
- William Sulzer of New York
- John Tener of Pennsylvania

The formal meeting during the afternoon wasn't the only one held in the Great Tent throughout the day. During the Grand Reunion, 65 reunions of regiments, brigades, divisions and corps took place there.

The Pennsylvania Reunion Commission reported that "these Reunions gave many hours of especial pleasure to our veteran guests, with their reawakenings of memories of the past, their renewals of friendships, their happy, unexpected meetings of comrades long separated and oft-times counted as 'gone beyond.'"[1]

Of course, these reunions didn't stop the veterans from meeting in other ways.

As the Grand Reunion rolled into its third day, the veterans continued to meet and reminisce about their days of glory.

W. M. Swope, a member of the 4th Virginia Regiment, was standing in Blocher's Jewelry Store in Gettysburg when he started speaking with Harry White of Greencastle, Pa. During their conversation about the reunion, they each took off their hats showing that both of them had head wounds. When the two men compared notes, they discovered that they had both been wounded at Dunkard Church during the Battle of Antietam on the same day and in the same way. "Their friendship immediately started to extend and before the day was over they felt as though they had known each other all their lives," reported the *Gettysburg Times*.²

Veterans wait to mail postcards at the temporary post office. *(Scanned from the Pennsylvania Reunion Commission report)*

Helen Longstreet, the widow of the Confederate General Longstreet, acted as a correspondent for the *New York Times* during the reunion writing about her thoughts, impressions and observations. She noted:

"By every train day and night for the last six days the republic's scarred heroes have poured into this quaint, sleepy town in the hills of Pennsylvania, this tilt yard of American chivalry. The crippled legions who stood behind the guns on these Pennsylvania battle heights, the broken ranks who charged across the valleys, now white and peaceful under Summer suns, once more tread the streets of Gettysburg. In the gray dawns and purple twilights of these July days America listens as they march on, to the tramp, tramp of the Old Guard. The men who were at Gettysburg when the Peach Orchard was a field of blood and Cemetery Ridge was a peak of fire are at Gettysburg again, and for the last time perhaps."³

New York Governor William Sulzer attended and spoke at the Grand Reunion. *(Courtesy Wikimedia Commons)*

However, the veterans had also noticed how few of their friends and comrades were actually at the reunion. Time and death had taken so many of them. Though it was the largest reunion of its kind with 54,000 veterans attending, more than three times that number had fought in the battle 50 years earlier.

A sense of melancholy hung over the events. A Pennsylvanian who actually lived in Gettysburg was standing next to a cherry tree on the battlefield. He recalled he had been standing in the same place 50 years earlier with a young soldier from Michigan

Veterans enjoying the sightseeing at the Grand Reunion at Gettysburg. *(Courtesy of the Library of Congress)*

whom he had liked.

"The young Michigan soldier was little more than a lad; dark-haired, dark-eyed, slender, and straight as an Indian," the veteran recalled. "Them Michigan boys were great fighters. The Michigan boy soldier was the bravest of the brave. He talked to me a great deal about the sweetheart he had left behind. He told me of eyes blue as the heavens above, and fair hair that held of gleams of sunlight and throat and cheeks like the magnolias we had picked away down in Old Virginia."[4]

On July 3, 1863, the Michigan boy had received a letter from his girl. Then came Pickett's Charge and the Union Army's desperate repulse of the attack.

"The repulse of Pickett's division made all of us feel that the end was in sight and that the Nation's flag would still wave over land and sea, with the star of every truant State shining in its undimmed blue," the veteran recalled.[5]

The Pennsylvanian and the Michigan boy were resting not far from the cherry tree.

"I picked a quart of cherries and traded them to him for three pieces of hard tack; as he was eating the cherries, a stray shell directed by the Devil snuffed out the life of Michigan's boy soldier. I took from his pocket the picture of the little girl who was waiting in her faraway Michigan home and sent it back to her

Left and above: Veterans enjoying some down time at the reunion. *(Courtesy of the Library of Congress and scanned from the Pennsylvania Reunion Commission report)* Below: One of the state groups represented the Confederate veterans. *(Courtesy of the Library of Congress)*

with a lock of her dead soldier's hair. It was the women who suffered most during the war, and I am sorry they are not here today," the Pennsylvanian said.[6]

Overall, the reunion had gone well and the organizers were feeling quite proud. Even the weather was now cooperating with the storm of the day before. The oppressive high temperatures had fallen back to more pleasing warm temperatures.

"Gettysburg has done itself proud. It is probable that there are few, if any, instances in which a town this size has been confronted with a proposition such as that which presented itself this week to Gettysburg, and it is certainly true that no town or city ever had a celebration of such magnitude and passed through it with such little difficulty and such absolute satisfaction to all concerned," the *Gettysburg Times* bragged.[7]

## FEW DEATHS

Though heat and age had kept the personnel in the medical tents busy during the reunion, the veterans had proved surprisingly hardy.

Union and Confederate veterans at the High Water Mark monument at Gettysburg *(Courtesy of the Soldier's Museum)*

"So remarkable is this low record of mortality among a body of 40,000 or 50,000 men, practically all of whom are over 70 years of age, that it was felt for a day or two that the authorities were keeping from the public the actual condition of affairs," the *Gettysburg Times* reported.[8]

One of the Gettysburg reunion's speakers talks to a group on the battlefield. *(Courtesy of the Library of Congress)*

Dr. Samuel G. Dixon, Pennsylvania Commissioner of Health, said that the old soldiers had survived so well at the reunion because, "In the first place the old soldiers represent the survival of the fittest. Secondly the sanitary arrangements for the celebration were considered with the utmost care and have been of the most advanced character."[9]

He complimented the quality of the hospital service at the camp and the skill of the nurses and physicians. "Both in the city and encampment prompt and constant attention of experienced physicians and nurses has been all given all ailing veterans and civilians, lifting many of them out of the jaws of death. This has unquestionably served many who would have under any other circumstances sunk into death," Dixon said.[10]

One of the veterans who suffered from heat exhaustion is loaded onto an ambulance. *(Courtesy of the Library of Congress)*

## SAYING THANKS

During the afternoon's formal meeting, Colonel Andrew Cowain called once again for the creation of the Peace Memorial that had been dropped from the reunion events. Other memorials had been dedicated during the reunion however, such as the William Wells statue.

Henry M. Couden, chaplain of the U.S. House of Representatives, said during the meeting, "We thank Thee that peace is stronger than war, justice than injustice, mercy than revenge, love than hate. We are met on a great battlefield where men fought each other to death fifty years ago, but now we meet in fraternity and love, rejoicing in the victory of the Blue and the Gray."[11]

During the day, the Virginia contingent of veterans led by General J. Thompson Brown walked two miles through the Great Camp. They stopped in front of the tent of Major J. E. Normoyle, the quartermaster in charge of the camp. On behalf of the veterans, Brown said:

> "Maj. Normoyle, the soldiers from Virginia come here tonight to present

Above: The remaining Confederate veterans recreate Pickett's charge 50 years later. Below: Union and Confederate veterans from Pickett's charge shake hands across the wall. *(Photos courtesy of the Library of Congress)*

thanks to you for the great way in which you have treated the Confederates, and from the bottom of their hears they extend their utmost compliments and good wishes. Only a man of your type could have done what you accomplished. When the government selected you to take charge of the arrangements of this camp, the greatest of its kind the world had ever known, it selected a man whose equal is not to be found every day."[12]

Normoyle had tears in his eyes as he stood at attention to receive the praise. When Gen. Brown finished, he turned to General Hunter Liggett, the camp commander, and apologized for paying honor

Left: A group of veteran musicians playing a song. *(Courtesy of the Library of Congress)* Below: Special guests at the reunion talking about the events of the day. *(Courtesy of the Library of Congress)* Below left: A group of veterans reminiscing about the battle of Gettysburg. *(Scanned from the Pennsylvania Reunion Commission report)*

# No North, No South...

Scenes from the reunion of veterans at the Bloody Angle. *(Courtesy of the Library of Congress)*

to Normoyle in the presence of a superior officer. Moved by the display of affection he had just seen, Liggett simply said, "No harm done."[13]

## PICKETT'S LAST CHARGE

The highlight of July 3 was a replay of Pickett's Charge using the surviving veterans who had come to the reunion. The two lines formed a quarter mile apart. The Philadelphia Brigade stood the north and Pickett's Division on the south side of the stone wall, over which they had fought so desperately fifty years earlier.

"There were no flashing sabers, no guns roaring with shell, only eyes that dimmed fast, and kindly faces behind the stone wall that marks the angle. At the end, in place of wounds or prison or death, were handshakes, speeches, and mingling cheers."[14]

From the thousands of men who had made the daring charge in 1863, only 150 Confederate soldiers remained to repeat the charge.

"They came up the slope in columns of fours, irregular, but responsive to the commands of Maj. W.W. Bentley, of the Twenty-fourth Virginia, one of the few officers of either Pickett's or the Philadelphia brigade who was present."[15]

They were led by a marching band. The veterans carried a faded Confederate flag "its red field pierced with many holes, its crossbars dim, and its shaft colored with the sweat of many and died that it might fly high in that last desperate effort to pierce the Union lines."[17]

The aged men gathered to either side of the battlefield; the Confederates to the west and Union to the east. The Confederates moved across the battlefield at a slow pace.

"It's progress was slow and painful, for the timothy of the field was high and its plowed surface was not easy for world weary feet. Up to the very edge of the stone wall, covered now with tangled vines and shaded by trees, they marched in

### Recollections

One of the Civil War veterans from Illinois recounted this story for a reporter:

*As we rode through Gettysburg that last time, I remember a little girl stopped my horse and said she wanted to give me a bouquet. I got down, and she pinned a ribbon—a little purple ribbon, to my coat. "Wear that in the next battle you get into," she said.*

*"We're not going to have any more battles around here," I told her.*

*"Yes, you are," she insisted. "Those hills back there are full of rebels."*

*I wore that purple ribbon through the battle. I never saw the girl afterward; but I've kept the ribbon, and it's back at home in Illinois today.*[16]

the hot sun while the band played 'Dixie'."[18]

Rep. J. Hampton Moore, of Philadelphia, a congressman from the 3rd Pennsylvania District, presented on behalf of the Philadelphia Brigade Association to the Pickett's Division Association a beautiful silk flag of the United States.

The report of the Pennsylvania Reunion Commission described it this way:

> "During the address, the standard bearers of the two flags first mention advanced midways between the two lines, crossing their flag staffs, and at its conclusion the standard bearer of the silken emblem of our United country, unfurling it on the Stone Wall, ran forward and held it above the two bat-
>
>
>
> Veterans greeting each other at the Grand Reunion. *(Scanned from the Pennsylvania Reunion Commission Report)*
>
> tle flags, while Comrade Bentley, in words of eloquence and patriotism, accepted it on behalf of the Picket's Division Association, immediately after which the two lines were advanced to the stone fence, and the identical men,-- their heads silvered, some with empty sleeves and others on crutches—who half a century before had fought over it with bayonets and butts of muskets, clasped hands and buried their faces on each other's shoulders, while a might shout of praise burst forth from the thousands of interested spectators who had caught the spirit of the occasion.

A group of veterans swap stories while sitting around the Great Camp. *(Courtesy of the Library of Congress)*

These battle-scarred veterans were there to swear allegiance to their country's flag, and to dedicate themselves anew to the Union. Their fraternization will not only be an epoch in this country, but will be felt across the sea."[19]

## FIREWORKS

The evening of July 3 featured a large fireworks display shot off from the top of Little Roundtop that cost an estimated $10,000.[20]

"The display began with a wonderfully well arranged electric display which lighted the sky like the bursting of bombs as the cannon roared. This continued for fully 10 minutes, with the burning of red and blue light in such quantities that the sky for miles and miles around was lighted. then the electrical display was temporarily stopped and only read and blue lights were burned."[21]

Among the features was a 200-foot-wide by 120-foot-tall American flag and a figure of a Union and Confederate soldier shaking hands. It included 100 pyrotechnists who shot off 4,000 shells ranging in diameter from 3 to 30 inches.[22]

"Perhaps the most interesting feature of the entire display—the one that will bring the thrill of the days of '61 to the veterans who have been spared for this great reunion—will be the exact reproduction of the signal code of the Union

Union and Confederate veterans putting aside their differences at Gettysburg.
*(Courtesy of the Library of Congress)*

Union and Confederate veterans put aside their differences at Gettysburg. *(Courtesy of U. S. Militaria Forums)*

Army—sixteen set pieces in red, white and blue fire. Radiant in gorgeous fire will also burn the corps badges of the Army of the Potomac and that of the Confederate forces identified with the Gettysburg battle."[23]

The flag display was released from a special balloon shell so that the flag floated over the veterans.[24]

An estimated 14,000 cars packed into the area filled with spectators who wanted to see the fireworks. The Pennsylvania Reunion Commission report noted that they double parked along both sides of every from in the area and when their headlights were turned on, it "seemed as though thousands of gigantic fireflies were silently, swiftly moving through the darkness of night, throughout the great battlefield's length and breadth..."[25]

The U.S. Cavalry and Pennsylvania State Police directed the traffic that did not clear out until well after midnight.

The sound of the show was so loud that it frightened many of the veterans. A few of the veterans were thrown back to 1863 and started shouting, "Down, boys! Lie down! Steady."[26]

Batavia resident Alvin J. Fox fought in Lockwood's Brigade during the Battle of Gettysburg. "The sounds of the firing of aerial bombs and the explosion of fireworks last Thursday night reminded him, he said, of the sounds of battle," *The Daily News* reported.[27]

Top: North Carolina veterans resting on the battlefield at Gettysburg. (*Courtesy of the Edgecombe County Memorial Library*) Above: Veterans touring the Gettysburg battlefield. (*Scanned from the Pennsylvania Reunion Commission report*)

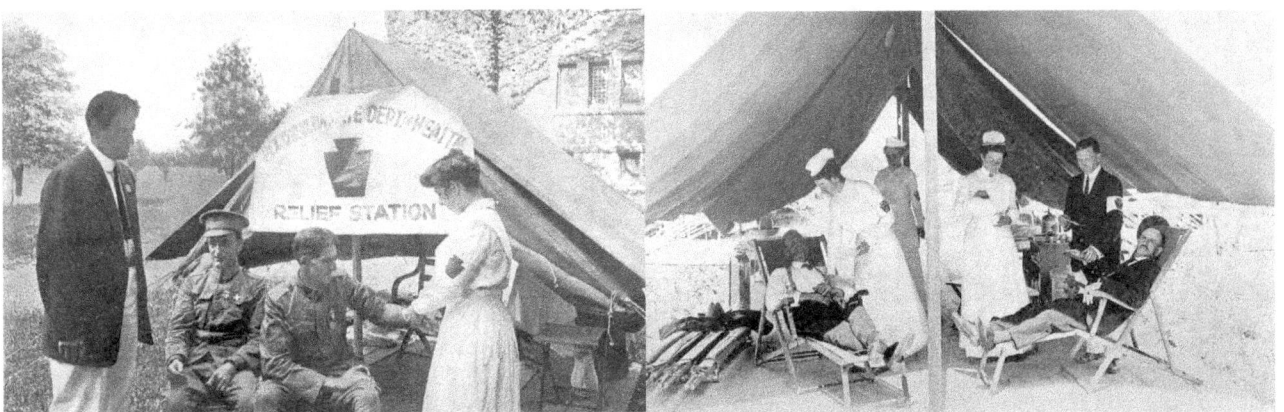

# Casualties at the Gettysburg Reunion

During the 50th Reunion of the Battle of Gettysburg, nine veterans died. Eight had served in the Union Army and one had been a Confederate soldier. A temporary morgue was established in Gettysburg to hold the dead bodies until they could be returned to their hometowns.

| Name | Hometown | Age | Condition |
|---|---|---|---|
| Allen D. Albert | Washington D.C. | 69 | Cerebral hemorrhage |
| Augustus D. Brown | Livermore Falls, Maine | 73 | Heart failure |
| Henry H. Hodges | Union Hill, N.C. | 70 | Cardiac dilation |
| John Reynolds | Portchester, N.Y. | 69 | Acute cardiac dilation |
| Edgar Rigsby | Wauwatosa, Wis. | 68 | Astenis |
| Otto L. Stam | Almond, N.Y. | 75 | Apoplexy |
| George M. Walls | Lewistown, Pa. | 69 | Acute uremia |
| Christopher Yates | Latrobe, Pa. | 78 | Heart prostration |

Scenes of the Great Camp medical staff at work. (*Photos courtesy of the Library of Congress*)

# 7

# NATIONAL DAY
# JULY 4, 1913

Though the actual Battle of Gettysburg ended on July 3, 1863, the reunion commission had added a fourth day to the official activities. July 4, 1913, was "National Day" at the Grand Reunion. What better way to celebrate the peace and unity among former enemies than to have both sides join in the celebration of united country?

During the day, Judge Alfred Beers, commander-in-chief of the Grand Army of the Republic met with a Confederate veteran from Kentuckian. The man told him, "Do you know, Judge, you people have us to be thankful to, for settling the question of the indissolubility of the Union. And it's for this reason. If we couldn't defeat you, there's no country on earth could. And think what a proposition a foreign foe would be up against to attack us as a united nation."[1]

The special speaker on this final day was President Woodrow Wilson. He arrived from Baltimore at the Gettysburg train station at 11 a.m. "His appearance at the station of Gettysburg was the signal for a cheer and from down in the Gettysburg College grounds came a 21-gun salute," the *New York Times* reported.[2] Wilson, Gov. Tener, U.S. Representative Mitchell Palmer and their entourage drove through town and out to the Great Camp.

At the camp, his car passed between two rows of Boy Scouts to reach the main tent. As Wilson entered the tent in his black frock coat, "Hail to the Chief" played and an estimated 10,000 people, both Union and Confederate veterans, stood up and cheered him. The speaker's platform was filled with Pennsylvania government officers, Union and Confederate Army representatives and women.

Wilson was a good choice for speaker. Not only was he the current commander-in-chief of the United States military, but his father had owned slaves and briefly served in the Confederate Army as a chaplain. One of Wilson's earliest memories had been hearing that Abraham Lincoln had been elected president, which meant that war was coming.[3]

Gov. Tener took to the podium and introduced the President. Wilson stood up and spoke slowly and carefully while "the breeze that played under the side of the tent and the restless feet of those who hastened in made it difficult for the old men in the

President Wilson arrives at the Gettysburg reunion. *(Courtesy of the Library of Congress)*

rear seats to hear and understand. He was interrupted only once or twice with cheering and that seemed perfunctory."[4]

The response to the Wilson's speech was also mixed. "Some who spoke unfavorably of it referred to Lincoln's address at the same place on Nov. 19, 1863, but most confined their comments to an expression of opinion that the President had not been in camp long enough to catch the sentiment that prevailed. Their view was, 'It's a good speech and ought to have been made at some other place, but not at Gettysburg,'" reported the *New York Times*.[5]

It was said that the speech failed to inspire and contained few phrases that stuck in the memory.[6] He praised the veterans for their service, saying that they had set an example for the nation. He said the veterans were looking to the current generation to "perfect what they had established. Their work is handed unto us, to be done in another way but not in another spirit."[7]

He then went on to say what the nation faced then was greater than what it had faced 50 years earlier.

> "We have harder things to do than were in the heroic days of war, because harder to see clearly, requiring more vision, more calm balance of judgment, a more candid searching of the very springs of right.
>
> "Look around you upon the field of Gettysburg! Picture the array, the fierce heat and agony of battle, column hurled against column, battery bellowing to battery! Valor! Yes! Greater no man shall see in war; and self-sacrifice, and loss to the uttermost; the high recklessness of exalted devotion which does not count the cost.
>
> "We are made by these tragic, epic things to know what it costs to make a

President Wilson speaks to the veterans at the Gettysburg reunion. *(Courtesy of the Library of Congress)*

President Wilson boarding the train at Gettysburg. *(Courtesy of the Library of Congress)*

nation—the blood and sacrifice of multitudes of unknown men lifted to a great stature in the view of all generations by knowing no limit to their manly willingness to serve."[8]

The speech lasted about half an hour. Afterwards, he shook hands with many of the people on the platform and then walked to his car between two lines of Pennsylvania State Troopers. He was driven back to town and got on the train to Harrisburg. He had been in Gettysburg for all of 46 minutes.

The gathered crowd to listen to a speech at the Gettysburg reunion. *(Courtesy of the Library of Congress)*

## Comparing meals between 1863 and 1913

Comparing sample menus that the veterans ate at Gettysburg in 1863 and 1913.

|  | 1863 | 1913 |
|---|---|---|
| **Breakfast** | Hardtack, beans, bacon, coffee | Puffed rice, fried eggs, cream potatoes, bacon, fresh bread, hard bread, butter, coffee |
| **Supper** | Hardtack, beans, bacon, coffee | Fricasseed chicken, peas, corn, ice cream, cake, cigars, fresh bread, hard bread, butter, coffee |
| **Dinner** | Hardtack, beans, bacon, coffee | Salmon salad, macaroni and cheese, butter fresh bread, coffee |

Army bakers prepare fresh bread for the veterans at the Great Camp. *(Courtesy of the Adams County Historical Society, Gettysburg, PA)*

# 8

# GOODBYES

Breakfast on Saturday, July 5, was the last meal served in the Great Camp. The exodus from the camp began soon after the meal. New friends and old acquaintances said their goodbyes and exchanged addresses as they packed their bags and headed into Gettysburg walking along the dusty Emmitsburg Road.

Others made one last visit to the battlefield to find a memento.

"Bits of things found on the battlefield proved to be the mementoes of many. One veteran was seen making home a tiny pine tree in a small crock; another had a sprout from a willow tree which he claimed had saved his life during the battle; others took along branches of canes, and note has already been made of the veteran from Iowa who carried home two suitcases full of ground from the scene of Pickett's Charge."[1]

Jefferson Sefton of Dubuque, Iowa, was the veteran who took home two suitcases of soil from the battlefield.

"This is more precious to me than anything else. I fought on the spot where I gathered this soil, and I want to take some of it back home. I shall make a garden box of it," Sefton said.[2]

As the church bells tolled noon, bugles sounded throughout the Great Camp and the members of the Pennsylvania Commission, Gen. Liggett and his staff and the guests at the college and seminary stood at attention as the colors at each location were lowered to half-staff.

"Immediately all over the great battlefield, wherever they are at the moment, Veteran guests, in Blue and in Gray, Regular Army officers, visitors, Boy Scouts, enlisted men and civilian employees, likewise stand at 'Attention.' In the distance a battery commences firing the National Salute. The for full five minutes as regularly, faintly boom the distant guns, all over that great plain, on wooded ridge and open slope, in shaded valley and rocky den, silently, reverentially, the highest and the humblest, thus pay each his tribute to those thousands who fifty years before on that self same plain, 'midst war's most fearful setting,' there 'gave the last full measure of devotion' to the cause each believed was right."[3]

The salute ended, the bugles sounded again and the flags were raised to full-staff while the bands played the National Anthem to mark the end of the Grand Reunion.

Now the work of getting the veterans home and dismantling the tent city began. It was expected that it would take two months before the ground where the Grand Reunion had been would be restored back to its original condition.[4]

"All day long weary veterans walked over the dusty roads and streets to the railroad stations in the big camp and in the town of Gettysburg and stood or sat around under the rays of a scorching sun while the trains to take them home were being prepared," according to the *New York Times*.[5]

Once the veterans arrived at the train station, they had to wait patiently until a man with a megaphone announced each train being made up and ready for boarding. Each departing train was made up, on average, of a dozen cars.

"Carrying with them happy memories and the satisfaction of having spent a week of celebration with no cause for regret veterans from every section of the United States are now wending their way homeward to tell to their friends the story of the greatest anniversary celebration in the world's military history."[6]

The day was hot, possibly the most-uncomfortable of the day. One Confederate veteran from North Carolina, H. H. Hodges, became the last veteran to die during the reunion. The 70-year-old veteran passed away on July 5 from heart failure.[7]

The doctors and nurses running the first aid stations in the camp were pleased with how well the veterans had handled the heat. "Instead of the hundreds of patients they expected, the hospitals are practically bare, and the hospital cars that were sent here for the transportation of sick veterans will go away empty," according to the *New York Times*.[8]

A few patients still remained in the emergency hospital in Gettysburg. Seven men were still too ill to go home on the last day and were

## Reunion Attendees

The official attendance reported by the Pennsylvania Reunion Commission:

| | |
|---|---:|
| Civil War Veterans | 53,407 |
| Officers | 124 |
| War Department Men Assigned to Administer the Camp | 1,342 |
| Newspaper Reporters | 155 |
| Cooks, Kitchen Helpers, Bakers and Laborers | 2,170 |
| **Grand Total** | **57,198** |

taken to a hospital in Harrisburg.⁹

Though 54,000 is the oft-quoted figure for how many veterans attended the reunion, the New York State Commission for the reunion estimated it as 70,000 with 55,000 of them staying in the camp.

By Saturday evening, many if not most of the veterans were gone. The streets in the Great Camp were deserted except for workers whose job it was to dismantle to the camp.

The Great Camp closed for good on July 7. The Boy Scouts marched through Gettysburg, headed by the 3rd Regiment Band, and took a special train back to Philadelphia. The State Police left that morning off to new duties. The State Health Department had left the previous day. The final meal had been served and the extra firefighting equipment kept in the camp returned to Harrisburg.⁹

Veterans board trains to head home from the Gettysburg reunion. *(Courtesy of the Library of Congress)*

Above: Veterans boarding one of the trains for home. Below: The ambulance that transported ill veterans to medical care during the Grand Reunion. *(Photos courtesy of the Adams County Historical Society, Gettysburg, PA)*

# Medical Care During the Gettysburg Reunion

**Cases For Emergency Relief:**

| | |
|---|---|
| Disorders of the digestive system | 2223 |
| Moderate exhaustion from heat and over exertion | 149 |
| Minor accidents and injuries | 109 |
| Tonsillitis and throat affections | 37 |
| Conjunctivitis | 18 |
| Aggravated sunburn | 17 |
| Severe migraines | 15 |
| Cystitis, and retention of urine | 6 |
| Poison Ivy | 6 |
| Asthma | 4 |
| Edema of the lower extremities and varicose veins | 3 |
| Furunculosis | 3 |
| Abscesses | 3 |
| Rheumatism | 2 |
| Hernia | 2 |
| Hemorrhoids | 2 |
| Insect Stings | 2 |
| Tuberculosis | 1 |
| Epilepsy | 1 |
| *TOTAL* | *603* |

**Admitted and stayed overnight:**

| | |
|---|---|
| Heat exhaustion | 226 |
| Diarrhea and intestinal disorders | 52 |
| Accidental injuries | 48 |
| Exhaustion from excitement and over exertion | 39 |
| Acute indigestion and gastric disturbances | 16 |
| Rheumatism | 6 |
| Bronchitis | 3 |
| Dermatitis following sunburn | 2 |
| Poison ivy | 2 |
| Chronic constipation | 2 |
| Laryngitis | 1 |
| Bite of insect | 1 |
| Ulcer of the leg | 1 |
| Prolonged migraine | 1 |
| Hernia | 1 |
| Angina pectoris | 1 |
| Arteriosclerosis | 1 |
| Infected wound of the hand | 1 |
| Foreign body in the eye | 1 |
| Tuberculosis | 1 |
| *TOTAL* | *406* |

**Admissions to State Emergency Hospital :**

| | |
|---|---|
| Heat Exhaustion | 319 |
| Exhaustion, Physical | 116 |
| Diseases, digestive | 69 |
| Alcoholism | 59 |
| Diarrhea | 55 |
| Diseases, circulatory | 31 |
| Diseases, nervous | 23 |
| Injuries | 16 |
| Diseases, genito-urinary | 15 |
| Constipation | 10 |
| Bronchitis | 9 |
| Rheumatism | 8 |
| Diseases, respiratory | 6 |
| Diseases, cutaneous | 4 |
| Malaria | 2 |
| Tonsillitis | 1 |
| Sunstroke | 1 |
| *TOTAL* | *744* |

# 9

# EPILOGUE

The Grand Reunion wasn't the last great reunion of Gettysburg and Civil War veterans, but it was the last time that such a large number of veterans gathered in one place. Just as 50 years had thinned the ranks of the veterans in 1913, another 25 years only reduced them more. The country fought in World War I, enjoyed the Roaring 20's and endured the Great Depression. With the ending of World War I, the country also had a new generation of veterans, some of whom had even attended to the needs of the Civil War veterans during the 1913 reunion.

"By the 1930's, a new generation of veterans from the Great War outnumbered the old veterans of the past, largely forgotten in time as their numbers dwindled and more pressing affairs touched American lives. A more radical and less forgiving leadership altered the United Confederate Veterans, and with time the goodwill expressed at the 1913 reunion was just a faint memory."[1]

## THE 75TH REUNION

As 1938 and the 75th anniversary of the Battle of Gettysburg approached, it seemed doubtful that another reunion would take place. However, Gettysburg native Paul Roy spent five years working to convince veterans groups, business leaders and politicians about the need for one last benchmark reunion.

In 1935, the Pennsylvania legislature once again created a commission to organize the reunion. The federal government entered into the planning the following year when the U.S. House Military Affairs Committee recommended the Haines Bill to work with the Pennsylvania Reunion Commission.

Though the event came together, only 1,800 veterans (1,356 Union veterans and 486 Confederate veterans) turned out for the reunion from among an estimated 8,000 living Civil War veterans.[2] It made it quite obvious that this would be the last great reunion of Civil War veterans. Those veterans who did attend were generally in their 90's.

The veterans began arriving in Gettysburg on June 29 when 12 special Pullman trains arrived in Gettysburg.[3]

July 1 was Reunion Day with the opening exercises held at the Gettysburg College Stadium that included the Secretary of War Harry Hines Woodring, chairman of the United States Commission.[4]

An aerial view of the crowd gathered to for the dedication of the Eternal Light Peace Memorial in 1938. *(Courtesy of Wikimedia Commons)*

The second day was Veterans' and Governors' Day. It featured a three-mile-long parade and a performance of the Marine Corps Band at the Gettysburg College stadium.[5]

July 3 was President's Day. The veterans attended a memorial service at the college stadium. Veterans also shook hands across the stone wall at the angle in the same way they had at the 1913 Gettysburg Reunion. A quarter million people attended the dedication of the Eternal Light Peace Memorial and more than 100,000 were stuck in their cars on the highways.[6] President Franklin D. Roosevelt spoke for nine minutes and at sunset the memorial was covered by a 50-foot flag.[7] The Army Air Corp staged a simulated air raid on Gettysburg at dusk and searchlights were directed from the ground at the planes while they dropped flares.

The last day of the reunion was United States Army Day that featured tank maneuvers and an air show. The day ended with a searchlight display.[8]

The veterans' camp during the reunion had been at the north end of Gettysburg College and some of the surrounding private property.[9]

The U.S. Treasury minted 50,000 commemorative half dollars in order to raise funds for the reunion. They were dated 1936, though they weren't minted until 1937. The coins sold for $1.65 and featured Union veteran James Power Stanley of the Battles of the Wilderness, Cold Harbor and Spotsylvania for the model.[10]

The 75th Reunion was considered by many the last reunion of Civil War veterans. It was certainly the last major reunion. The few remaining Civil War veterans quickly died off in the coming years.

The specially minted 50-cent piece for the 75th Battle of Gettysburg Reunion in 1938.

## THE LAST VETERANS

The final veterans of the Confederate States armed forces died in the 1950s. A number of men claimed to be last remaining Confederate veteran. These men died throughout the 1950's. Many of their claims were debunked as more information about their births was uncovered. The largest problem in verifying their claims was that many Confederate records had been destroyed or lost because the Confederate government had no official archive system.

Pleasant Crump died at the end of 1951 at the age of 104. He was the oldest of the group of Confederate veterans who had a verified service record.

Crump was an Alabamian. Near the end of the Civil War, he and a friend traveled to Petersburg, Virginia, and enlisted in the 10th Alabama Infantry in November 1864. He saw action at the Battle of Hatcher's Run and participated in the siege of Petersburg. He was also present at General Robert E. Lee's surrender at Appomattox Court House.

Crump returned to Alabama and married Mary Hall. They had five children. Hall died in 1901 and Crump married Ella Wallis in 1905. She died in 1942.

The United Confederate Veterans awarded him the honorary rank of colonel in 1950.

The last Union veteran was Albert Woolson, who died in 1956 at the age of 109.[11] He had been born in 1847 in Antwerp, N.Y.

Albert's father had enlisted in the Union Army and was wounded in the Battle of Shiloh. His wounds were treated at an army hospital in Windom, Minn., but he eventually died. Not before Albert and his mother had moved there to be close to him.

After Albert's father died, Albert joined the 1st Minnesota Heavy Artillery Regiment

Albert Woolson, the last Civil War veteran.

as a drummer boy on August 10, 1864. He never saw any action and was discharged on September 7, 1865.

Woolson returned to Minnesota after his discharge. He became a member of the Grand Army of the Republic and even rose to the position of senior vice commander in chief in 1953.

He died of lung congestion in Duluth, Minn. on August 2, 1956, and was buried with full military honors at Park Hill Cemetery.

President Dwight D. Eisenhower said, following Woolson's death, "The American people have lost the last personal link with the Union Army ... His passing brings sorrow to the hearts of all of us who cherished the memory of the brave men on both sides of the War Between the States."[12]

Soldiers' National Cemetery. *(Courtesy of the Library of Congress)*

# ENDNOTES

## CHAPTER 1: HENRY S. HUIDEKOPER

1. Lieutenant Colonel Thomas Chamberlin, *History of the Fiftieth Regiment Pennsylvania Volunteers, Second Regiment, Bucktail Brigade* (Philadelphia, PA: F. McManus, Jr. & Co., 1905) p. 117; http://files.usgwarchives.net/pa/1pa/military/cwar/150-bucktails/bucktail-14.txt

2. *Ibid.*

3. Chamberlin, p. 118.

4. Chamberlin, p. 119.

5. Chamberlin, p. 130.

6. Chamberlin, p. 131.

7. eHistory Archive: Civil War Battlefield Surgery, http://ehistory.osu.edu/uscw/features/medicine/cwsurgeon/amputations.cfm

8. James W. Wensyel, "Testaments to the Past: Return to Gettysburg", *American History Illustrated*, July/August 1993, p. 42.

9. E.F. Moody Life Expectancy Tables, http://www.efmoody.com/estate/lifeexpectancy.html

## CHAPTER 2: THE PENNSYLVANIA BATTLE OF GETTYSBURG COMMISSION

1. *Fiftieth Anniversary of the Battle of Gettysburg, Report of the Pennsylvania Commission* (Harrisburg, PA: William Stanley Ray, State Printer, 1913) p. 178.

2. Barbara L. Platt, *"This is holy ground" A history of the Gettysburg Battlefield 1863-2009* (Harrisburg, PA: Huggins Printing, 2009) p. 8.

3. *New York Times*. John Reed Scott, "How Veterans and Others Will Be Cared For at Gettysburg," June 29, 1913.

4. *Report of the Pennsylvania Commission*, p. 3.

5. *Report of the Pennsylvania Commission*, pp. 4-5.

6. *Report of the Pennsylvania Commission*, p. 6.

7. *Report of the Pennsylvania Commission*, p. 6

8. *New York Times.* Unsigned article. "The First Southern State Monument at Gettysburg," April 13, 1913.

9. Stone Sentinels: State of Virginia Monument, http://www.gettysburg.stonesentinels.com/Confederate/Va.php

10. *Report of the Pennsylvania Commission,* p. 7.
11. Thomas' Legion: The Great Gettysburg Reunion of 1913, http://thomaslegion.net/thegreatgettysburgreunionof1913.html
12. Thomas' Legion: The Great Gettysburg Reunion of 1913, http://thomaslegion.net/thegreatgettysburgreunionof1913.html
13. *Report of the Pennsylvania Commission,* p. 12.
14. *New York Times.* Unsigned article. "Provides for Veterans," June 24, 1913.
15. *Report of the Pennsylvania Commission,* p. 24.
16. *Report of the Pennsylvania Commission,* p. 15.
17. *Report of the Pennsylvania Commission*, p. 45.
18. *Report of the Pennsylvania Commission*, p. 228.
19. *Report of the Pennsylvania Commission,* p. 228.
20. *Gettysburg Compiler,* Unsigned article. "Pennsylvania Monument," August 17, 1910.
21. *Gettysburg Times.* Unsigned article. "Commission selects site," February 25, 1909.
22. *New York Times.* John Reed Scott, "How Veterans and Others Will Be Cared For at Gettysburg," June 29, 1913.
23. *New York Times.* John Reed Scott, "How Veterans and Others Will Be Cared For at Gettysburg," June 29, 1913.
24. *New York Times.* Unsigned article. "Veterans of North and South to Unite Again At Gettysburg," February 19, 1913.
25. *Report of the Pennsylvania Commission,* p. 48.
26. *Gettysburg Times.* Unsigned article. "A Gloomy View," June 16, 1913.
27. The American Review of Reviews. Unsigned Article. "Horse Versus Automobile: A French View," September 1910. http://www.oldmagazinearticles.com/how_many_cars_were_there_in_1910_pdf
28. *Washington Post.* Unsigned article. "Auto Routes to Gettysburg; One Going, One Returning," June 22, 1913.
29. *Report of the Pennsylvania Commission,* p. 65.
30. *Washington Post.* Unsigned article. "Mr. Heflin at Gettysburg," May 31, 1913.
31. *New York Times.* Unsigned article. "Wilson to Gettysburg," June 29, 1913.
32. *Sunday Review* (Decatur, IL). Unsigned article. "Wilson will go to Gettysburg," June 29, 1913.
33. *New York Times.* Unsigned article. "Veteran Vanguard Now in Gettysburg," June 29, 1913.
34. Frank N. Britchner Collection scrapbook. Unsigned article. "Stars and Bars Absent From Union Camp." The Frank N. Britchner Collection scrapbook is part of the Adams County (Pa.) Historical Society collection. It is part of a donation by a pharmacist who lived in Gettysburg at the time of the reunion. The scrapbook is a collection of articles written during the 1913 Grand Reunion. Many come from the *Baltimore American*, but many others have been clipped from the newspaper and so the origin is uncertain. I have included article titles, dates and authors where available.
35. *The Indianapolis News.* Unsigned article. "The Gettysburg Reunion," March 29, 1913.
36. *Washington Post.* Unsigned article. "Blue and Gray Will Unite on Plains of Gettysburg," May 22, 1913.
37. *Meadeboro the Tented Village,* 1913 brochure, National Park Service.
38. *Adams County News.* Unsigned article. "Many Students Will Be Here," June 7, 1913.
39. *Adams County News.* Unsigned article. "Many Students Will Be Here," June 7, 1913.

## CHAPTER 3: ARRIVING

1. *The Indianapolis News.* Unsigned article. "The Second Gettysburg," July 4, 1913.
2. *New York Times.* Unsigned article. "Veteran Vanguard Now in Gettysburg," June 29, 1913.
3. *Gettysburg Times.* Unsigned article. "First Boys in Gray Are Here," June 26, 1913.
4. *Report of the Pennsylvania Commission,* p. 52.
5. *Gettysburg Times.* Unsigned article. "Artillery Here for Celebration," June 27, 1913.

6. *The Daily News*. Mark Graczyk, "Hidden History: A Civil War reunion in Gettysburg, 1913," July 3, 2011. http://thedailynewsonline.com/blogs/mark_my_words/article_fe7a4d58-9ba4-11e0-8784-001cc4c03286.html

7. *New York Times*. Unsigned article. "Veteran Vanguard Now in Gettysburg," June 29, 1913.

8. *New York Times*. Unsigned article. "Veteran Vanguard Now in Gettysburg," June 29, 1913.

9. *Gettysburg Times*. Unsigned article. "Stories of the old veterans," June 27, 1913.

10. *Baltimore American*. Lester Mueller. "Veteran's Long Walk to Camp," July 3, 1913.

11. *New York Times*. Unsigned article. "Veteran Vanguard Now in Gettysburg," June 29, 1913. However, other reports listed 46 or 48 states, though no counts given.

12. *Baltimore American*. Lester Mueller. "Veteran's Long Walk to Camp," July 3, 1913.

13. *Washington Post*. Unsigned article. "Going to Gettysburg," June 29, 1913.

14. *Washington Post*. Unsigned article. "Going to Gettysburg," June 29, 1913.

15. *Washington Post,* Unsigned article. "Civil War Veterans Whose Deeds Will Be Glorified at Gettysburg," June 28, 1913.

16. *Washington Post*. Unsigned article. "Vanguard in Camp," June 30, 1913.

17. *Washington Post*. Unsigned article. "Going to Gettysburg," June 29, 1913.

18. *New York Times*. Unsigned article. "Veteran Vanguard Now in Gettysburg," June 29, 1913.

19. *Report of the Pennsylvania Commission*, p. 89.

20. *New York Times*. Unsigned article. "Heat Prostrates Gettysburg Host," June 30, 1913.

21. *New York Times*. Unsigned article. "Heat Prostrates Gettysburg Host," June 30, 1913.

22. *Washington Post*. Unsigned article. "Going to Gettysburg," June 29, 1913.

23. *New York Times*. Unsigned article. "Veteran Vanguard Now in Gettysburg," June 29, 1913.

24. *Gettysburg Times*. Unsigned article. "Over 40,000 now in camp," July 1, 1913.

25. Thomas' Legion: The Great Gettysburg Reunion of 1913, http://thomaslegion.net/thegreatgettysburgreunionof1913.html

26. *Washington Post*. Unsigned article. "25,000 Veterans Already on Historic Battlefield," June 30, 1913.

27. *Washington Post*. Unsigned article. "Old Foes in Tears," July 1, 1913.

28. *Washington Post*. Unsigned article. "Tented City at Gettysburg Where Crippled and Aged Warriors of Past are Encamped, Reveling in Reminiscences and Awaiting Bugle Call That Will Inaugurate Celebration," July 1, 1913.

29. *New York Times*. Unsigned article. "Heat Prostrates Gettysburg Host," June 30, 1913.

30. Frank N. Britchner Collection scrapbook. Unsigned article. "Hundreds Visit Sickles."

31. *Washington Post*. Unsigned article. "Tented City at Gettysburg Where Crippled and Aged Warriors of Past are Encamped, Reveling in Reminiscences and Awaiting Bugle Call That Will Inaugurate Celebration," July 1, 1913.

32. *Washington Post*. Unsigned article. "Gen. Sickles Refuses to Take $1,000 from Thaw," July 4, 1913.

33. *Roanoke Beacon* (Plymouth, NC). Unsigned article. "With Blue and Gray at Gettysburg," July 11, 1913.

34. *Gettysburg Times*. Unsigned article. "Veterans Here By Thousands," June 30, 1913.

35. Frank N. Britchner Collection scrapbook. Unsigned article. "Taken By Surprise at Night."

36. *Gettysburg Times*. Unsigned article. "Over 40,000 now in camp," July 1, 1913.

37. Frank N. Britchner Collection scrapbook. Unsigned article. "Taken By Surprise at Night."

38. *Gettysburg Times*. Unsigned article. "Over 40,000 now in camp," July 1, 1913.

39. *Washington Post*. Unsigned article. "25,000 Veterans Already on Historic Battlefield," June 30, 1913.

40. *Washington Post*. Unsigned article. "25,000 Veterans Already on Historic Battlefield," June 30, 1913.

41. *Report of the Pennsylvania Commission*, p. 67.
42. *Adams County News*. Unsigned article. "Many Students Will Be Here," June 7, 1913.
43. *Gettysburg Times*. Unsigned article. "Veterans Here By Thousands," June 30, 1913.
44. *The Washington Post*. Unsigned article. "At Gettysburg," June 30, 1913.
45. *Baltimore American*. Lester Mueller. "Every Detail is Complete," June 28, 1913.
46. *Baltimore American*. Lester Mueller. "Every Detail is Complete," June 28, 1913.
47. *New York Times*. Unsigned article. "Gettysburg Honor to Girls of '63," July 1, 1913.
48. *New York Times*. Unsigned article. "Gettysburg Honor to Girls of '63," July 1, 1913.
49. *Report of the Pennsylvania Commission*, p. 49.
50. *1915 Spectrum Yearbook* of Gettysburg College (Gettysburg, PA), p. 156.
51. *1915 Spectrum Yearbook* of Gettysburg College (Gettysburg, PA), p. 156.
52. *1915 Spectrum Yearbook* of Gettysburg College (Gettysburg, PA), p. 156.
53. *1915 Spectrum Yearbook* of Gettysburg College (Gettysburg, PA), p. 157.
54. *New York Times*. Unsigned article. "Gettysburg Honor to Girls of '63," July 1, 1913.
55. Wensyel, James W. "Testaments to the Past: Return to Gettysburg." *American History Illustrated*, July/August 1993, p. 45.
56. *New York Times*. Unsigned article. "Old Soldiers Defy Gettysburg Heat," July 2, 1913.
57. Wensyel, James W. "Testaments to the Past: Return to Gettysburg." *American History Illustrated*, July/August 1993, p. 45.
58. Wensyel, James W. "Testaments to the Past: Return to Gettysburg." *American History Illustrated*, July/August 1993, p. 45.
59. Wensyel, James W. "Testaments to the Past: Return to Gettysburg." *American History Illustrated*, July/August 1993, p. 46.
60. *New York Times*. Unsigned article. "Veteran Vanguard Now in Gettysburg," June 29, 1913.
61. *New York Times*. Unsigned article. "Veteran Vanguard Now in Gettysburg," June 29, 1913.
62. Thomas' Legion: The Great Gettysburg Reunion of 1913, *http://thomaslegion.net/thegreatgettysburgreunionof1913.html*
63. Thomas' Legion: The Great Gettysburg Reunion of 1913, *http://thomaslegion.net/thegreatgettysburgreunionof1913.html*
64. *New York Times*. Unsigned article. "Veteran Vanguard Now in Gettysburg," June 29, 1913.
65. *The Philadelphia Evening Bulletin*. Unsigned article. "The Men of Gettysburg," June 30, 1913.
66. *New York Times*. Unsigned article. "Gettysburg Honor to Girls of '63," July 1, 1913.
67. *New York Times*. Unsigned article. "Gettysburg Honor to Girls of '63," July 1, 1913.
68. *New York Times*. Unsigned article. "Gettysburg Honor to Girls of '63," July 1, 1913.
69. *New York Times*. Unsigned article. "Gettysburg Honor to Girls of '63," July 1, 1913.
70. *New York Times*. Unsigned article. "Gettysburg Honor to Girls of '63," July 1, 1913.
71. *New York Times*. Unsigned article. "Gettysburg Honor to Girls of '63," July 1, 1913.
72. *New York Times*. Unsigned article. "Gettysburg Honor to Girls of '63," July 1, 1913.

## CHAPTER 4: VETERANS' DAY - JULY 1, 1913

1. Wensyel, James W. " Testaments to the Past: Return to Gettysburg." *American History Illustrated*, July/August 1993, p. 46.
2. *New York Times*. Unsigned article. "Old Soldiers Defy Gettysburg Heat," July 2, 1913.
3. Wensyel, James W. "Testaments to the Past: Return to Gettysburg." *American History Illustrated*, July/August 1993, pp. 45-6; *New York Times*. Unsigned article. "Old Soldiers Defy Gettysburg Heat," July 2, 1913.

4. Wensyel, James W. "Testaments to the Past: Return to Gettysburg." *American History Illustrated*, July/August 1993, p. 47.

5. Wensyel, James W. "Testaments to the Past: Return to Gettysburg." *American History Illustrated*, July/August 1993, p. 47.

6. Wensyel, James W. "Testaments to the Past: Return to Gettysburg." *American History Illustrated*, July/August 1993, pp. 47-8.

7. Wensyel, James W. "Testaments to the Past: Return to Gettysburg." *American History Illustrated*, July/August 1993, p. 48.

8. *Gettysburg Times*. Unsigned article. "Reunions on Battlefield," July 1, 1913.

9. *Gettysburg Times*. Unsigned article. "Veterans here but few others," July 1, 1913.

10. *Gettysburg Times*. Unsigned article. "Chance for local husband hunters," June 2, 1913.

11. *Gettysburg Times*. Unsigned article. "Veteran Marries," July 1, 1913.

12. *Report of the Pennsylvania Commission*, p. 95.

13. *Report of the Pennsylvania Commission*, p. 96.

14. *Report of the Pennsylvania Commission*, p. 98.

15. *Report of the Pennsylvania Commission*, p. 101.

16. *Report of the Pennsylvania Commission*, p. 101.

17. *Report of the Pennsylvania Commission*, p. 111.

18. Haines, John W. "The Fiftieth Anniversary Celebration of the Battle of Gettysburg." *The Lincoln Herald*, Winter 1953.

19. U.S. Army Quartermaster Museum: This Week in Quartermaster History July 9-15, *http://www.qmmuseum.lee.army.mil/historyweek/9-15jul.htm*

20. U.S. Army Quartermaster Museum: This Week in Quartermaster History July 9-15, *http://www.qmmuseum.lee.army.mil/historyweek/9-15jul.htm*

21. U.S. Army Quartermaster Museum: This Week in Quartermaster History July 9-15, *http://www.qmmuseum.lee.army.mil/historyweek/9-15jul.htm*

22. Frank N. Britchner Collection scrapbook. Unsigned article. "Big Figures."

23. Haines, John W. "The Fiftieth Anniversary Celebration of the Battle of Gettysburg." *The Lincoln Herald*, Winter 1953.

24. *Washington Post*. Unsigned article. "Gettysburg Saloons Are Now Closed at 10:30 p.m.," July 2, 1913.

25. *Washington Post*. Unsigned article. "Incidents on Gettysburg Battlefield During Second Day of Big Encampment," July 2, 1913.

## CHAPTER 5: MILITARY DAY - JULY 2, 1913

1. *New York Times*. Unsigned article. "Seen By Mrs. Longstreet," July 3, 1913.

2. *Gettysburg Times*. Unsigned article. "Out of Window," July 2, 1913.

3. *Gettysburg Times*. Unsigned article. "Bury the Hatchet," July 2, 1913.

4. *Gettysburg Times*. Unsigned article. "Took Off His Arm," July 2, 1913.

5. *Gettysburg Times*. Unsigned article. "Missed His Shot," July 2, 1913.

6. Thomas' Legion: The Great Gettysburg Reunion of 1913, *http://thomaslegion.net/thegreatgettysburgreunionof1913.html*

7. *Washington Post*. Unsigned article. "Veterans Defy Sun," July 2, 1913.

8. *Washington Post*. Unsigned article. "Veterans Defy Sun," July 2, 1913.

9. Jarvis, Craig. "Triangle trio buys massive painting." *The News & Observer* (Raleigh, NC) May 2, 2007.

10. *New York Times*. Unsigned article. "Tented Gettysburg Swept by Storm," July 3, 1913.

11. *New York Times*. Unsigned article. "Tented Gettysburg Swept by Storm," July 3, 1913.

12. *New York Times*. Unsigned article. "Stabbed at Gettysburg," July 3, 1913.

13. Silent Era: The Battle of Gettysburg, *http://www.silentera.com/PSFL/data/B/BattleOfGettysburg1913.html*

## CHAPTER 6: CIVIC DAY - JULY 3, 1913

1. *Report of the Pennsylvania Commission*, p. 133.
2. *Gettysburg Times,* Unsigned article. "Strange Meeting," July 6, 1913.
3. *New York Times*. Unsigned article. "Seen By Mrs. Longstreet," July 3, 1913.
4. *New York Times*. Unsigned article. "Seen By Mrs. Longstreet," July 3, 1913.
5. *New York Times*. Unsigned article. "Seen By Mrs. Longstreet," July 3, 1913.
6. *New York Times*. Unsigned article. "Seen By Mrs. Longstreet," July 3, 1913.
7. *Gettysburg Times*. Unsigned article. "Gettysburg May Well Be Proud," July 6, 1913.
8. *Gettysburg Times*. Unsigned article. "Low Death Rate Among Veterans," July 2, 1913.
9. *Gettysburg Times*. Unsigned article. "Low Death Rate Among Veterans," July 2, 1913.
10. *Gettysburg Times*. Unsigned article. "Low Death Rate Among Veterans," July 2, 1913.
11. *Report of the Pennsylvania Commission*, p. 135.
12. *Washington Post*. Unsigned article. "3,000 Virginians Join In Tribute to Maj. Normoyle," July 4, 1913.
13. *Washington Post*. Unsigned article. "3,000 Virginians Join In Tribute to Maj. Normoyle," July 4, 1913.
14. *Washington Post*. Unsigned article. "Gray Men Totter to Bloody Angle," July 4, 1913.
15. *Washington Post*. Unsigned article. "Gray Men Totter to Bloody Angle," July 4, 1913.
16. Frank N. Britchner Collection scrapbook. Unsigned article. "From song to story."
17. *Washington Post*. Unsigned article. "Gray Men Totter to Bloody Angle," July 4, 1913.
18. *News and Observer* (Raleigh, NC). Josephus Daniels, Jr. "Half Flag Found After 50 Years," July 4, 1913.
19. *Report of the Pennsylvania Commission*, p. 171.
20. Frank N. Britchner Collection scrapbook. Unsigned article. "Great Fireworks Display."
21. Frank N. Britchner Collection scrapbook. Unsigned article. "Great Fireworks Display."
22. *Gettysburg Times*. Unsigned article. "Taft Will Take Wilson's Place," June 17, 1913.
23. *Gettysburg Times*. Unsigned article. "Taft Will Take Wilson's Place," June 17, 1913.
24. *Gettysburg Times*. Unsigned article. "Taft Will Take Wilson's Place," June 17, 1913.
25. *Report of the Pennsylvania Commission,* p. 172.
26. Wensyel, James W. "Testaments to the Past: Return to Gettysburg." American History Illustrated (July/August 1993) p. 50.
27. Thomas' Legion: The Great Gettysburg Reunion of 1913, http://thomaslegion.net/thegreatgettysburgreunionof1913.html

## CHAPTER 7: NATIONAL DAY - JULY 4, 1913

1. *Gettysburg Times*. Unsigned article. "Stories of the old veterans," June 27, 1913.
2. *New York Times*. Unsigned article. "Gettysburg Cold to Wilson's Speech," July 5, 1913.
3. Presidential Avenue.com: Woodrow Wilson 28th President, 1913-1921, *http://www.presidentialavenue.com/ww.cfm*
4. *New York Times*. Unsigned article. "Gettysburg Cold to Wilson's Speech," July 5, 1913.
5. *New York Times*. Unsigned article. "Gettysburg Cold to Wilson's Speech," July 5, 1913.
6. *New York Times*. Unsigned article. "Gettysburg Cold to Wilson's Speech," July 5, 1913.
7. *Report of the Pennsylvania Commission*, p. 175.
8. *ibid.*

## CHAPTER 8: GOODBYES

1. *Gettysburg Times*. Unsigned article. "Few Veterans Remain Here," July 6, 1913.
2. *Report of the Pennsylvania Commission*, p. 177.

3. *New York Times*. Unsigned article. "Gettysburg Camp All But Deserted," July 6, 1913.

4. *New York Times*. Unsigned article. "Gettysburg Camp All But Deserted," July 6, 1913.

5. *Gettysburg Times*. Unsigned article. "Few Veterans Remain Here," July 6, 1913.

6. *Report of the Pennsylvania Commission*, p. 56.

7. *New York Times*. Unsigned article. "Gettysburg Camp All But Deserted," July 6, 1913.

8. *Report of the Pennsylvania Commission*, p. 12.

9. *Gettysburg Times*. Unsigned article. "Veterans' Camp Finally Closed," July 7, 1913.

## CHAPTER 9: EPILOGUE

1. Thomas' Legion: The Great Gettysburg Reunion of 1913, *http://thomaslegion.net/ thegreatgettysburgreunionof1913.html*

2. Frank N. Britchner Collection scrapbook. Unsigned article. "Camp Aftermath."

3. Salmon, John S (2007) (Google Books). *Historic Photos of Gettysburg* (Nashville, TN: Turner Publishing Company, 2007) p. 171.

4. *New Oxford Item* (New Oxford, PA). Unsigned article. "Local News," June 23, 1938.

5. *Reading Eagle* (Reading, PA). Unsigned article. "Blue, Gray Veterans Gather At Gettysburg for Reunion," June 29, 1938.

6. *The Rock Hill Herald* (Rock Hill, SC). Unsigned article. "Men of Sixties Review Parade," July 2, 1938.

7. Gettysburg National Military Park: Virtual Tour-Day One: Oak Hill "Peace Eternal in a Nation United," *http://www.nps.gov/archive/gett/getttour/ tstops/tstd-03.htm*.

8. *Reading Eagle* (Reading, PA). Unsigned article. "Throng at Gettysburg Hears Roosevelt Call For Peace Campaign," July 4, 1938.

9. Cohen, Stan B. *Hands Across the Wall*. (Charleston, WV: Pictorial Histories Pub. Co., 1982) p. 45.

10. Cohen, Stan B. *Hands Across the Wall*. (Charleston, WV: Pictorial Histories Pub. Co., 1982) p. 41.

11. *Prescott Evening Courier* (Prescott, AZ). Unsigned article. "Veteran Poses for Commemorative Coin," May 24, 1938.

12. In mid-2006, new census research indicated that Albert Woolson was actually only 106 years old, being listed as less than one year old in the 1850 census. Previous research in 1991 has suggested he was a year younger than claimed (108 instead of 109), although this does not affect his veteran status.

13. *St. Petersburg Times* (St. Petersburg, FL). Unsigned article. "Last 24 Hours," August 3, 1956.

# About the Author

James Rada, Jr. is the author of seven novels, two non-fiction books and two non-fiction collections. These include the historical novels *Canawlers, October Mourning, Between Rail and River* and *The Rain Man*. His other novels are *Logan's Fire, Beast* and *My Little Angel*. His non-fiction books are *Saving Shallmar: Christmas Spirit in a Coal Town, Battlefield Angels: The Daughters of Charity Work as Civil War Nurses, Looking Back: True Stories of Mountain Maryland* and *Looking Back II: More True Stories of Mountain Maryland*.

He lives in Gettysburg, Pa., where he works as a freelance writer. Jim has received numerous awards from the Maryland-Delaware-DC Press Association, Associated Press, Maryland State Teachers Association and Community Newspapers Holdings, Inc. for his newspaper writing.

If you would like to be kept up to date on new books being published by James or ask him questions, he can be reached by e-mail at *jimrada@yahoo.com*.

To see James' other books or to order copies on-line, go to *www.jamesrada.com*.

**PLEASE LEAVE A REVIEW**

If you enjoyed this book, please help other readers find it. Reviews help the author get more exposure for his books. Please take a few minutes to review this book at Amazon.com or Goodreads.com. Thank you, and if you sign up for my mailing list at jamesrada.com, you can get FREE ebooks.

If you liked

# NO NORTH, NO SOUTH...

you can find more stories at these FREE sites from

## JAMES RADA, JR.

---

### JAMES RADA, JR.'S WEB SITE

*www.jamesrada.com*

The official web site for James Rada, Jr.'s books and news including a complete catalog of all his books (including eBooks) with ordering links. You'll also find free history articles, news and special offers.

---

### TIME WILL TELL

*historyarchive.wordpress.com*

Read history articles by James Rada, Jr. plus other history news, pictures and trivia.

---

### WHISPERS IN THE WIND

*jimrada.wordpress.com*

Discover more about the writing life and keep up to date on news about James Rada, Jr.

www.ingramcontent.com/pod-product-compliance
Lightning Source LLC
Chambersburg PA
CBHW051213290426
44109CB00021B/2436